NABI

The Prophetic Heavenly Ascension

MI'RAAJUN NABI

The Prophetic Heavenly Ascension

سُبْحَٰنَ الَّذِي أَسْرَىٰ بِعَبْدِهِ لَيْلًا مِّنَ الْمَسْجِدِ الْحَرَامِ

إِلَى الْمَسْجِدِ الْأَقْصَى الَّذِي بَارَكْنَا حَوْلَهُ لِنُرِيَهُ مِنْ آيَاتِنَا

إِنَّهُ هُوَ السَّمِيعُ الْبَصِيرُ

SHAYKH FAIṢAL ḤĀMID 'ABDUR-RAZĀK

Al-Faisaliyyah
PRESS

In the name of Allāh,

the Most Gracious, the Most Merciful

يا رَبِّ بِالمُصْطَفى بَلِّغْ مَقاصِدَنا
وَاغْفِرْ لَنا ما مَضَى يا وَاسِعَ الكَرَمِ

YA RABBI BIL MUṢṬAFĀ BALLIGH MĀ QAṢIDANA
WAGHFIRLANA MA MAḌA YĀ WĀSI ʿAL KARAMI

O My Lord, for the sake of the Chosen One (Your Beloved Prophet and Our Master Muḥammad ﷺ), let us attain all that we are hoping for. And pardon us for what has passed. (O Allah) The Most Bountiful and Generous One.

Miʿraajun Nabi: *The Prophetic Heavenly Ascension*

For more information, contact Islamic Forum of Canada, Brampton, Ontario, Canada

www.IslamicForum.ca

Author:	Shaykh Faisal Hamid Abdur-Razak
Published by:	Al-Faisaliyyah Press
First Edition:	1988
Second Edition:	February 2023
ISBN:	978-1-7775814-6-6
E-mail:	Media@IslamicForumOnline.com
Telephone:	(905) 790-8859
Address:	Islamic Forum of Canada 200 Advance Boulevard Brampton, Ontario, L6T 4V4 Canada

DEDICATION

To My Late Grandfather *As-Sayyid Al-Shareef Al-Imam Abu Ḥamid Abdur-Razak Al-Ḥanafi (Raḥimahullāh).*
For his passionate Love for Islām and Muslims.

﴿رَّبِّ ٱرْحَمْهُمَا كَمَا رَبَّيَانِى صَغِيرًا﴾

RABBIR ḤAMHUMĀ KAMĀ RABBAYĀNĪ SAGHĪRĀ

"My Lord ! Bestow on them Your Mercy even as they cherished me in childhood."

(Sūrah Al-Israa', 17:24)

Arabic Transliteration Key

ى / ا	ā
ب	b
ت	t
ث	th
ج	j
ح	ḥ
خ	kh
د	d
ذ	dh
ر	r
ز	z
س	s
ش	sh
ص	ṣ
ض	ḍ
ط	ṭ
ظ	ẓ

ع	‘ (ayn)
غ	gh
ف	f
ق	g
ك	k
ل	l
م	m
ن	n
ه	h
و	w
ـُ	ū
ي	y, ī
ؤ / ء	’
أ / ـَ	a
إ / ـِ	i
ة	h
آ	āā

Glyph Key

ﷻ | سُبْحَانَهُ وَتَعَالَىٰ | *subḥanahu wa taʿālā* | Glory be to Allāh, the Exalted. Used when mentioning the name of Allāh ﷻ.

ﷺ | صَلَّى ٱللَّهُ عَلَيْهِ وَسَلَّمَ | *ṣallallāhu ʿalayhī wa sallam* | May the Peace and Blessings of Almighty Allāh be upon him. Used after mentioning the Holy Prophet Muḥammad 's ﷺ name.

عَلَيْهِمُ ٱلسَّلَامُ | عَلَيْهِمُ ٱلسَّلَامُ | *ʿalayhim as-salam* | Peace be upon them. An Honorific used at the mentioning of 3 or more Prophets, Messengers, or Angels.

عَلَيْهِ ٱلسَّلَامُ | عَلَيْهِ ٱلسَّلَامُ | *ʿalayhis salam* | Peace be upon him. An Honorific used at the mentioning of no more than one Prophet, Messenger, or Angel.

عَلَيْهَا ٱلسَّلَامُ | عَلَيْهَا ٱلسَّلَامُ | *ʿalayhas salam* | Peace be upon her. An Honorific used at the mentioning one of the mother, wives, or daughters of the Prophets, or a great pious woman in Islām.

عَلَيْهِمَا ٱلسَّلَامُ | عَلَيْهِمَا ٱلسَّلَامُ | *ʿalayhimas salam* | Peace be upon him. An Honorific used at the mentioning of two Prophets, Messengers, or Angels.

رَضِيَ ٱللَّهُ عَنْهُ | رَضِيَ ٱللَّهُ عَنْهُ | *raḍiyallāhu ʿanhu* | May Allāh be pleased with him. An honorific used at the mentioning of one male companion of the Messenger of Allāh ﷺ.

رَضِيَ ٱللَّهُ عَنْهَا | رَضِيَ ٱللَّهُ عَنْهَا | *raḍiyallāhu ʿanhā* | May Allāh be pleased with her. An honorific used at the mentioning of one female companion of the Messenger of Allāh ﷺ.

رَضِيَ ٱللَّهُ عَنْهُمَا | رَضِيَ ٱللَّهُ عَنْهُمَا | *raḍiyallāhu ʿanhuma* | May Allāh be pleased with them. An honorific used at the mentioning of exactly two companions of the Messenger of Allāh ﷺ.

رَضِيَ ٱللَّهُ عَنْهُمْ | رَضِيَ ٱللَّهُ عَنْهُمْ | *raḍiyallāhu ʿanhum* | May Allāh be pleased with them. An honorific used at the mentioning of more than two companions of the Messenger of Allāh ﷺ.

Contents

Acknowledgements

I gratefully acknowledge the contribution of many brothers and sisters towards the completion of this project.

Special mention must be made of Sayyid Muzzammil, Sidi Naeem Al-Faisal, Sidi Hussein Al-Faisal, Sidi Ammar Al-Faisal, Zubair Hakeem, and their families, and the many other brothers and sisters who assisted in one way or another, and the Sponsors of this Book Project.

I extend my sincere gratitude to my family. My wife Sayyidah Leem, and my children Sayyidah Maryam, Sayyid Muzzammil, Sayyidah Faatimah, Sayyid Ismail, and Sayyidah Khadijah.

I thank my beloved parents for their unceasing support, my sisters and their family, my late grandparents, my uncles, aunts, and my wife's family for their encouragement and support, and, last but not least, my wife and children for their sacrifice, love, patience and understanding.

I thank my Beloved Shaykh, His Eminence Al-'Allāmah As-Sayyid Al-Shareef, Shaykh Muḥammad Ibn Ibrahim Ibn Isma'il Al-Ya'qoubi Al-Hasani Al-Idrisi (Hafiẓahullāh) for his continued guidance and assistance. May Almighty Allāh ﷻ reward him and his noble family with the best of rewards.

Above all, I am eternally grateful to Almighty Allāh, subḥānahu wa ta'ālā, for the accomplishment of this work.

﴿وَمَا تَوْفِيقِيٓ إِلَّا بِٱللَّهِ﴾

"My success is only from Allāh."

(Sūrah Hūd, 17:24)

Introduction

أَعُوْذُ بِاللهِ مِنَ الشَّيْطَانِ الرَّجِيم

بِسْمِ ٱللَّهِ ٱلرَّحْمَٰنِ ٱلرَّحِيمِ ١

ٱلْحَمْدُ لِلَّهِ رَبِّ ٱلْعَٰلَمِينَ ٢ ٱلرَّحْمَٰنِ ٱلرَّحِيمِ ٣

مَٰلِكِ يَوْمِ ٱلدِّينِ ٤ إِيَّاكَ نَعْبُدُ وَإِيَّاكَ نَسْتَعِينُ ٥ ٱهْدِنَا ٱلصِّرَٰطَ ٱلْمُسْتَقِيمَ ٦

صِرَٰطَ ٱلَّذِينَ أَنْعَمْتَ عَلَيْهِمْ غَيْرِ ٱلْمَغْضُوبِ عَلَيْهِمْ وَلَا ٱلضَّآلِّينَ ٧

—

We praise and glorify Almighty Allāh who has made the sacred month of Rajab the month of Israa' and Mi'raaj, a glorious event in a blessed month.

The purpose of this book "*MI'RAAJUN NABI*", is to educate Muslims and Non-Muslims alike about the event of *Israa' wal Mi'raaj* – The Night Journey and Heavenly Ascension of the Messenger of Allāh, *ṣallahu 'alayhi wa sallam* – its impact on the Islamic *Ummah* (Nation), and the many lessons we can learn from this momentous and historic event.

The book deals with a wide range of topics relating to Al-Israa' Wal Mi'raaj and is divided into seven distinct parts containing a total of thirty-three chapters. This book can be read individually, or collectively in groups, with your family, relatives, and friends.

Part One contains a brief overview of the entirety of the events before, during, and after Al-Israa' Wal Mi'raaj.

Part Two elaborates on the events preceding Al-Israa' Wal Mi'raaj as well as the tribal composition of the Quraysh, and the preparation of Prophet Muḥammad ﷺ for this Miraculous Journey.

Part Three starts with an overview of the Journey by Night (*Al-Israa'*) as is narrated from the original sources. The following chapters in this part of the book deal in detail with the Journey of The Messenger of Allāh ﷺ from Masjidul Ḥaram in Makkah to Masjidul Aqṣā in Jerusalem and the events which transpired at Masjidul Aqṣā.

Part Four begins with an overview of the events of the Prophet's ﷺ ascension through the heavens (*Al-Mi'raaj*) as narrated from the original sources, followed by the details of Al-Mi'raaj, the visiting of The Prophet of Allāh ﷺ to Al-Baytul Ma'mūr – the Oft Visited House, Sidratul Muntahā – The Lote Tree Of The Utmost Boundary, the meeting of The Prophet Muḥammad ﷺ with his Lord, Almighty Allāh subḥānahu wa ta'āla, and their conversation (*Munājāt*). Part Four concludes with the descent of the Messenger of Allāh ﷺ and the events that occurred the morning after this Miraculous Journey of Al-Israa' Wal Mi'raaj.

Part Five deals with the aftermath and response of the inhabitants of Makkah making special note of the response of Sayyidunā Abū Bakr Aṣ-Ṣiddīq ؓ. Part Five concludes with a chapter on Obedience to Leadership as is revealed in the Qur'ān and in the authentic narrations (*Ḥadīth*) of Rasūlallāh may the Peace and Blessings of Allāh be upon him and his noble family.

Part Six gives a commentary on some important aspects of Al-Israa' Wal Mi'raaj: The Prophet's ﷺ vision of Almighty Allāh ﷻ, the relationship between Prophet Ibrāhīm ؑ, and Prophet Muḥammad ﷺ, the relationship between Prophet Mūsā ؑ and Prophet Muḥammad ﷺ, the importance of Ṣalāh and its position in the Islamic doctrine, the transfer of Prophethood from the

Israelites to the Arabs, and the socio-political dimensions of the Miʿraaj.

Part Seven, the final part of the book, concludes with the impact of Miʿraajun Nabi, including works of literature from various Scholars and Poets from Islamic History, the Miʿraaj in relation to science, and ways in which we can commemorate this Great Event of Miʿraajun Nabi.

The author of this book, our Noble Shaykh Faiṣal, went to Makkah in 1977 to do his formal Islamic Studies at Umm Al-Qura University. During these ten years in University, and in the subsequent years during his regular visits to Makkah, he would spend time with the Noble Shaykh His Eminence Sayyid Muḥammad Ibn ʿAlawī Al-Mālikī Al-Ḥasanī (Qaddasallāhu Sirrahu). Shaykh Faiṣal would recount how his visits to the Rusaifa District of Makkah, to the home and School of Shaykh Mālikī, were special moments to benefit from Shaykh Mālikī. This included the discussions of Shaykh Mālikī on the Israaʾ and Miʿraaj. Shaykh Faiṣal received many Ijāzahs from His Eminence Shaykh Muḥammad Ibn ʿAlawī Al-Mālikī.

It is our hope that this book, *MIʿRAAJUN NABI,* will help people understand the Israaʾ and Miʿraaj, and to appreciate the special status of the Noble Prophet Muḥammad ﷺ not only among other human beings, but among all of creation.

- S. Muzzammil Ibn Faiṣal Ḥāmid ʿAbdur-Razak
Toronto, Ontario, Canada
1444 / 2023

First Things First

Guidance From The Holy Qur'ān

Almighty Allāh reveals in the Holy Qur'ān:

﴿سُبْحَانَ الَّذِي أَسْرَىٰ بِعَبْدِهِ لَيْلًا مِّنَ
الْمَسْجِدِ الْحَرَامِ إِلَى الْمَسْجِدِ الْأَقْصَى
الَّذِي بَارَكْنَا حَوْلَهُ لِنُرِيَهُ مِنْ آيَاتِنَا ۚ إِنَّهُ هُوَ
السَّمِيعُ الْبَصِيرُ ۝١﴾

Glory be to Him (Allāh) who took His servant for the Journey by night from Masjidul Ḥarām (the Sacred Mosque in Makkah) to Masjidul Aqṣā (the Farthest Mosque in Jerusalem), whose precincts We have blessed. So that We might show him some of Our signs. Verily, He is the All-Hearing, the All-Seeing.

(Sūrah Al-Israa', 17:1)

بِسْمِ اللَّهِ الرَّحْمَنِ الرَّحِيمِ

وَٱلنَّجْمِ إِذَا هَوَىٰ ﴿١﴾

مَا ضَلَّ صَاحِبُكُمْ وَمَا غَوَىٰ ﴿٢﴾ وَمَا يَنطِقُ عَنِ ٱلْهَوَىٰٓ ﴿٣﴾

إِنْ هُوَ إِلَّا وَحْىٌ يُوحَىٰ ﴿٤﴾ عَلَّمَهُۥ شَدِيدُ ٱلْقُوَىٰ ﴿٥﴾

ذُو مِرَّةٍ فَٱسْتَوَىٰ﴿٦﴾ وَهُوَ بِٱلْأُفُقِ ٱلْأَعْلَىٰ﴿٧﴾ ثُمَّ دَنَا فَتَدَلَّىٰ﴿٨﴾

فَكَانَ قَابَ قَوْسَيْنِ أَوْ أَدْنَىٰ ﴿٩﴾ فَأَوْحَىٰٓ إِلَىٰ عَبْدِهِۦ مَآ

أَوْحَىٰ ﴿١٠﴾ مَا كَذَبَ ٱلْفُؤَادُ مَا رَأَىٰٓ ﴿١١﴾ أَفَتُمَٰرُونَهُۥ عَلَىٰ مَا

يَرَىٰ ﴿١٢﴾ وَلَقَدْ رَءَاهُ نَزْلَةً أُخْرَىٰ ﴿١٣﴾ عِندَ سِدْرَةِ ٱلْمُنتَهَىٰ ﴿١٤﴾

عِندَهَا جَنَّةُ ٱلْمَأْوَىٰٓ ﴿١٥﴾ إِذْ يَغْشَى ٱلسِّدْرَةَ مَا يَغْشَىٰ﴿١٦﴾

مَا زَاغَ ٱلْبَصَرُ وَمَا طَغَىٰ﴿١٧﴾

لَقَدْ رَأَىٰ مِنْ ءَايَٰتِ رَبِّهِ ٱلْكُبْرَىٰٓ ﴿١٨﴾

1. By the star when it goes down.
2. Your companion has neither gone astray nor has he erred.
3. Nor does he speak of (his own) desire.
4. It is no less than revelation sent down to him.
5. He has been taught by one mighty in power.
6. The Lord of Strength; so he attained completion,
7. While he was in the highest part of the horizon,
8. Then he approached and came closer,
9. And was at a distance of two bows' length or less.
10. So (Allāh) revealed to His servant whatever He revealed.
11. The heart lied not in what he saw.
12. Will you then dispute with him about what he saw
13. And indeed he saw him at a second descent.
14. Near Sidrat Al-Muntahā.
15. Near it is the Paradise of Abode.
16. When that covered the Lote Tree which did cover it!
17. The sight turned not aside, nor it transgressed beyond the limit.
18. Indeed he saw the greatest Signs of his Lord.

(Sūrah An-Najm, 53:1-18)

PART ONE

INTRODUCTION TO MIʿRAAJUN NABI

Chapter 1

Overview of Important Events

BEFORE THE MI'RAAJ

The Embargo Imposed By The Quraysh

From the Seventh year to the Tenth year of the Prophet's ﷺ mission. The Quraysh had imposed a boycott on Prophet Muḥammad ﷺ, his followers and supporters, including the entire clans of Banū Hāshim and Banū Al-Muṭṭalib. They were confined, with limited supplies to the Shi'b of Abū Ṭālib, a rugged, arid little valley on the outskirts of Makkah.

The Death Of Khadījah Bint Khuwaylid ؓ

Soon after the Prophet ﷺ settled in Makkah at the end of the boycott, his beloved wife, Khadījatul Kubrā ؓ, died.

The Death Of The Prophet's ﷺ Uncle Abū Ṭālib

A month and ten days after the death of Khadījah, Abū Ṭālib, the Prophet's ﷺ uncle and protector, passed away.

The Quraysh Intensified Their Persecution Of The Prophet ﷺ

Seeing an opportunity in the death of the Messengers Uncle, Abū Ṭalib, the Quraysh intensify their persecution on the Prophet of Allāh ﷺ and the believers.

The Trip To Ṭā'if

The Prophet directs his hopes for support, safety and protection to the city of Aṭ-Ṭā'if. They favoured their heathenistic sanctuary and their goddess, Al-Lāt, instead of the Message of Islam brought by the Prophet ﷺ. The elite of Ṭā-if hurled sardonic inquiries at the Prophet, and some of the inhabitants insulting and hurting him.

Return To Makkah From Ṭā'if

The Prophet ﷺ faced great difficulty in attempting to return back to Makkah from Ṭā-if as there was no one to protect him from the onslaught of the Quraysh

'Āmul Ḥuzn – The Year Of Grief

The year of the death of Abū Ṭalib and Khadījatul Kubrā ﵂ (raḍīallāhu 'anhā) became known as 'Āmul Ḥuzn – The Year of Grief.

DURING THE ISRAA'

Al-Israa' : The Night Journey From Makkah To Jerusalem

Mounted on the Burāq and accompanied by the Archangel Jibrīl ﵇ ('alayhis salām), the Messenger of Allāh ﷺ sets out on the first part of a Miraculous Journey.

Visit To Madīnah

Accompanied by the Archangel Jibrīl ﷺ the Prophet ﷺ visits a land called Ṭaybah (Madīnah), the prophesied land of Migration (Hijrah).

Visit To Damascus - Syria

The Prophet ﷺ visits Masjid Al-Umawi in Damascus, Syria. The land where Sayyidunā ʿIsā ﷺ (ʿalayhis salām) will return towards the end of time.

Visit To Egypt - (Sinai Peninsula)

The Prophet ﷺ visits the lands of Madyan and Sīna'.

Visit to Palestine - Bayt Laḥm

The Prophet ﷺ visits Bayt Laḥm in Palestine. The land of Sayyidunā ʿIsā ﷺ.

Events At Masjid Al-Aqṣā

DURING THE MIʿRAAJ

Al-Miʿraaj : The Bodily Ascension To Heaven

The Messenger of Allāh ﷺ ascends the Miʿraaj, meeting various Prophets and Messengers through his ascent to different levels of the heavens.

Al-Baytul Maʿmūr

The Messenger of Allāh ﷺ was taken to Al-Baytul Ma'mur.

Heaven And Hell

The Messenger of Allāh ﷺ is shown heaven and hell.

Sidratul Muntahā

The Messenger ﷺ was taken to the Lote Tree of the Utmost Boundary (Sidratul Muntahā).

In The Presence Of Almighty Allāh ﷻ

The Beloved of Allāh ﷺ meets and witnesses his Lord, the Almighty Allāh ﷻ, and is bestowed the command of Ṣalāh.

The Return Journey

The Messenger of Allāh ﷺ returns back to Makkah after this Miraculous Journey. The disbelievers of Quraysh attempted to discredit the event. However, Rasūlallāh ﷺ provides definitive proof as to the factualness of his journey.

PART TWO

PRELUDE TO MIʿRAAJUN NABI

Chapter 2
The Tribal Composition of Quraysh

We present here some useful information of the Tribal Composition of Quraysh. This will help to understand the political and social underpinnings of Makkan society.

Many of the responses of the people of Makkah to the Holy Prophet ﷺ, and to their daily affairs in general, were influenced by their Tribal affiliation and loyalty.

The Quraysh were divided into two Sections:[1]

1. The Quraysh of the Hollow
2. The Quraysh of the Outskirts

About 200 years before the birth of the Holy Prophet Rasūlallāh ﷺ, a Qurayshi named Qusayy married the daughter of Hulayl Ibn Ḥubshiyyah, the Tribal Chief of Khuzāʿah. Hulayl preferred his son-in-law (Qusayy – a non-Khuzāʿah) over his sons, as the Keeper

1 Seerah Ibn Hishām.

(Custodian) of the Ka'bah. This included the Key of the Door of the Ka'bah, so the Custodian would control both the entry and exit to the Ka'bah. They would be responsible for the Holy Sanctuary – a very important and influential position in Makkan society.

After Hulayl's death, a fierce power struggle ensued. Ultimately, Qusayy established himself as Ruler of Makkah in 440 CE, and brought his closest relatives to live near to him beside the Holy Sanctuary.

This group became known as the Quraysh of the Hollow. They lived in the Valley where the Ka'bah was located.[2] This group, the Quraysh of the Hollow, included the Clans of:

1. Qusayy
2. Zuhrah
3. Taym
4. Makhzūm

Qusayy's more remote tribesmen were pushed to the surrounding areas and became known as the Quraysh of the Outskirts. The Quraysh of the Outskirts included the Clans of:

1. 'Āmir
2. Sahm
3. 'Ādī
4. Ḥārith
5. Jumah

2 Seerah Ibn Hishām.

The Quraysh of the Hollow were divided into two Sections:

1. The Scented Ones
2. The Confederates

Towards the end of his life, Qusayy had to pick a successor from his four sons. Although ʿAbdu Manāf was the most capable, Qusayy chose his eldest son, Abd-ud-Dār, who was the least capable of the four sons. Qusayy chose him only because Abd-ud-Dār was his eldest son. This type of decision making was common in Arab culture. ʿAbdu Manāf accepted his father's wishes.

But in the next generation, more than half the Quraysh supported ʿAbdu Manāf's exceptional son Hāshim as their Tribal Leader. These included the Clans of Qusayy's younger three sons, and the Clans of Zuhrah and Taym. The Clans pledged their Allegiance (Bayʿah) to Hāshim by dipping their hands into perfume and rubbing them on the walls (stones) of the Kaʿbah. Since that day, those who supported Hāshim became known as the Scented Ones.[3]

The Clans who did not support Hāshim's leadership were ʿAbd-ud-Dār, Makhzūm, and some small outlying families. They continued to support ʿAbd-ud-Dār and became known as the Confederates. Tensions mounted between the two parties until they finally agreed to split Makkah's leadership roles. Hāshim would provide for the Pilgrims, while ʿAbd-ud-Dār would retain the Keys to the Kaʿbah.

3 Seerah Ibn Hishām.

The Scented Ones included the following Seven Clans:

1. Banū Hāshim
2. Banū Muṭṭalib
3. Banū Nawfal
4. Banū 'Abdu Shams
5. Banū Zuhrah
6. Banū As'ad
7. Banū Taym

The Confederates consisted of Two Clans:[4]

1. Banū Makhzūm
2. Banū 'Abd-ud-Dār

It is important to note that the Makhzūm Clan was the only Quraysh Clan of the Hollow that did not accept Hāshim leadership and continued to support 'Abd-ud-Dār. Even the Clan of Taym, which is just as distantly related as Makhzūm, acknowledged Hāshim's exceptional leadership.

The Makhzūm Clan became the most powerful Quraysh Clan at the turn of the Seventh century (C.E.), and continued to rebuff Hāshim's leadership. This is evidenced by their ruthless treatment of his great-grandson, the Holy Prophet Muḥammad ﷺ.

Abu Jahl, the fiercest enemy of the Prophet ﷺ, was from the Makhzūm Clan. Sayyidunā Abu Bakr, the greatest friend of the Prophet ﷺ, was from the Taym Clan.

4 Seerah Ibn Isḥāq

Chapter 3
Before the Israaʾ and Miʿraaj

The Details

There are some important events which took place prior to the Israaʾ and Miʿraaj.

1. Embargo

From the seventh year of the Prophet's ﷺ mission until the tenth year, the Quraysh imposed a boycott and embargo on the Prophet Muḥammad ﷺ, his followers and supporters, including the entire clans of Banū Hāshim and Banū Al-Muṭṭalib. They were banished from Makkah and confined, with limited supplies of food and necessities, to the Shiʿb of Abū Ṭālib, a rugged, arid little valley enclosed by hills on all sides. It could only be entered from Makkah by a narrow opening.

The Prophet ﷺ and his Followers endured much suffering and hardships. He saw the suffering of the Elderly, Women, and Children. It was a difficult time indeed for the Muslims.

2. Return To Makkah From The Embargo

Soon after the Prophet ﷺ settled in Makkah after the end of the boycott, two events took place that were particularly hard for his sensitive nature to bear.

3. Death Of Sayyidah Khadījah ﵂

First, Khadījah Bint Khuwaylid ﵂, the beloved wife of the Prophet ﷺ who had always helped and consoled him in times of hardship and distress, died unexpectedly. Her death left the Prophet ﷺ without the affectionate support which had for so long helped to sustain him in the face of trial and persecution. To the many sorrows and bereavements of his childhood there was now added this sad experience. Khadījah, faithful and loving Khadījah, his comfort, friend and companion, had now gone from his life. The Prophet ﷺ deeply grieved and, almost overwhelmed by sorrow, kept to his quarters for many days, rarely appearing in public.

4. Death Of Abū Ṭālib

A month and ten days after the death of Khadījah ﵂, Abū Ṭālib, his uncle and protector, passed away. The Prophet's ﷺ grief became even deeper. He kept more and more to his house, seldom venturing outside. He was keenly aware that he was left not only without a spouse, but also without a protector. His enemies saw in the death of Abū Ṭālib a long-awaited opportunity to intensify their persecution of the Prophet ﷺ without fearing the reprisal of Banū Hāshim now that their respected and influential patriarch had died. And this was precisely what happened.

5. Aggressive Persecution Of The Prophet ﷺ

'Abdullah Ibn 'Urwah Ibn Az-Zubayr on the authority of his father reported that the neighbours of the Prophet ﷺ who were opposed to him, under the leadership of Abū Lahab and his wife Umm Jamīl, intensified their campaign of persecution. The Prophet ﷺ used to remove the garbage which they repeatedly threw inside his yard and in front of his door, complaining in a markedly restrained voice:

"What kind of neighbourhood is this, O sons of 'Abd Manāf?"

Another terrible incident of persecution which the Prophet ﷺ experienced after the death of Abū Ṭālib is narrated by Ibn Isḥāq as follows :

> "Khadījah Bint Khuwaylid and Abū Ṭālib died in the same year. Misfortunes continue to befall the Messenger of Allāh ﷺ; much more than they dare to inflict upon him while Abū Ṭālib was alive.
>
> One of their insolent mobs even heaped dust upon his gracious head.
>
> As he entered the home, his loving daughter Fāṭimah cried passionately as she wiped the dust from her fathers blessed head. She was heartbroken seeing how the people were treating him.
>
> "Do not cry, my daughter," he said, "for Allāh is protecting your father."

6. Trip To Aṭ-Ṭā'if

After the people of Makkah had rejected his message, the Holy Prophet ﷺ directed his hopes and aspirations for support, safety and protection to the city of Aṭ-Ṭā'if. This city is located some sixty miles from Makkah, but, in contrast to the low altitude and excessively hot climate of the holy city, Aṭ-Ṭā'if lies at a high elevation, and enjoys a temperate climate. The city is in the midst of a green and fertile valley, famous for its vineyard. Since at that time many well-to-do Makkans had owned property in this valley and used the city as a summer resort to escape the harsh heat of Makkah.

So, only a few weeks after the deaths of Khadījah ﷺ and Abū Ṭālib, the Holy Prophet ﷺ set out for Aṭ-Ṭā'if, accompanied by Zayd ﷺ, his trusted adopted son. Once there, he went straight to a leading family of the city, the family of 'Amr Ibn 'Umayr Ath-Thaqafī. Three of the sons - 'Abd Yaleel, Mas'ūd, and Ḥabeeb - met with the Holy Prophet ﷺ and he invited them to embrace Islam and to worship Allāh ﷻ. But they impudently jeered at him and refused his invitation. They preferred their heathenistic sanctuary and their goddess, Al-Lāt, to the worship of the One True God. They asked the same pointless questions as their Makkan counterparts.

For ten days he stayed there delivering his message to several people, one after another, but to no avail.

Some of the people followed him, shouted abuse at him, hooted him through the alley-ways, pelted him with stones and forced him to flee the city, pursued by a relentless mob.

DU'Ā' OF THE PROPHET ﷺ AFTER VISIT TO ṬĀ'IF

اَللَّهُمَّ إِلَيْكَ أَشْكُو ضَعْفَ قُوَّتِى،

وَقِلَّةَ حِيْلَتِي،

وَهَوَانِي عَلَى النَّاسِ،

يَا أَرْحَمَ الرَّاحِمِيْنَ،

أَنْتَ رَبُّ الْمُسْتَضْعَفِيْنَ، وَأَنْتَ رَبِّيْ،

إِلَى مَنْ تَكِلُنِي؟

إِلَى بَعِيْدٍ يَتَجَهَّمُنِى؟ أَمْ إِلَى عَدُوٍّ مَلَّكْتَهُ أَمْرِيْ؟

إِنْ لَمْ يَكُنْ بِكَ عَلَيَّ غَضَبٌ فَلَا أُبَالِيْ،

وَلَكِنْ عَافِيَتُكَ هِيَ أَوْسَعُ لِيْ،

أَعُوْذُ بِنُوْرِ وَجْهِكَ الَّذِي أَشْرَقَتْ لَهُ الظُّلُمَاتُ،

وَصَلَحَ عَلَيْهِ أَمْرُ الدُّنْيَا وَالْآخِرَةِ مِنْ أَنْ تُنَزِّلَ بِيْ غَضَبَكَ،

أَوْ يَحِلَّ عَلَيَّ سَخَطُكَ،

لَكَ الْعُتْبَى حَتَّى تَرْضَى،

وَلَا حَوْلَ وَلَا قُوَّةَ إِلَّا بِكَ

O Allah! To You alone I complain of my weakness,
Of my inability (limited ability, insufficient ability).
and my insignificance before the people.
You are the Most Merciful One.
You are the Lord of the helpless and the weak.
O My Lord! Into whose hands would You entrust me:
Unto some distant stranger who will ill-treat me,
Or unto the enemy who has been given control over my affairs.
But if You are not angry with me,
I do not care about how people treat me.

Your forgiveness is enough for me.
I seek protection in the Light of Your Countenance,
which illuminates all darkness,
And fixes the affairs of this world and the Hereafter.
May it never be that I should incur Your wrath,
or that You should be angry with me.
To You I submit, until I earn Your Pleasure.
And there is no power and no might, except through You."

7. 'Ām Al-Ḥuzn - The Year Of Grief

The year in which Khadījah Bint Khuwaylid and Abū Ṭālib died became known as 'Ām Al-Ḥuzn (The Year Of Grief), because of the tremendous loss to the already afflicted Prophet ﷺ.

The Muslims shared in their leader's sorrow and mourning, but they were too weak and oppressed to provide the kind of protection he had lost due to the death of Abū Ṭālib.

Chapter 4
Training And Preparing The Prophet ﷺ For Israa' And Mi'raaj

Since birth and childhood, the Holy Prophet Muḥammad ﷺ had been carefully nurtured by Almighty Allāh ﷻ for his role as Final Prophet and Chosen Messenger.

An important aspect of this training was the spiritual and physical operation he had undergone.

1. The First Operation
When he was a child of no more than four years, staying with his bedouin wet-nurse, Ḥalīmah As-Sa'dīyah, the Angel Jibrīl ﷺ operated on the Holy Prophet ﷺ. This was witnessed by his foster brother, the son of Ḥalīmah As-Sa'dīyah.

2. The Second Operation
When he received the First Revelation of the Holy Qur'ān on Jabal Nūr, in the Cave of Ḥirā', the Angel Jibrīl ﷺ performed the Second Operation on the Holy Prophet ﷺ.

3. The Third Operation

Al-Ḥāfiẓ Ibn Kathīr reports accounts of Israaʾ and Miʿraaj which relate that Jibrīl ﷺ performed another operation at the beginning of the event of Al-Israaʾ wal Miʿraaj.

The Angel Jibrīl ﷺ took the Prophet ﷺ from the house of Umm Hāni to Al-Ḥaṭeem near the Kaʿbah. He opened the Prophet's ﷺ chest on the side of the heart, washed it with the water of Zamzam in a golden basin, and filled it with wisdom and mercy, and then put it back in its place.

This operation and training qualified the Prophet ﷺ to withstand the rigours and trials of Israaʾ and Miʿraaj. His ordinary human perceptive and cognitive powers would not have been able to withstand the power and illumination of Allāh ﷻ.

PART THREE

AL-ISRAAʾ: THE PROPHETIC JOURNEY BY NIGHT

Chapter 5

The Journey From Masjidul Ḥarām To Masjidul Aqṣā: An Overview Of The Events

The Events as Narrated in the Original Sources

There are many Authentic traditions from the Holy Prophet Muḥammad ﷺ concerning the ISRAA' AND MI'RAAJ contained in Ṣaḥīḥ Al-Bukharī and Ṣaḥīḥ Muslim and other reliable collections of Ḥadith. The Prophet ﷺ described this miraculous experience in the following words:

In The Home Of Umm Hāni

"I was one night sleeping at Makkah in the house of Umm Hāni, daughter of Abū Ṭālib and a sister of 'Alī, when Jibrīl ﷺ came to me.

Al-Haṭīm

He (The Archangel Jibrīl ﷺ) rent the roof of the house and brought me to Al-Haṭīm near the Ka'bah. He opened my chest on the side of the heart, washed it with the water of Zamzam in a golden basin, filled it with wisdom and mercy, and put it back in its place.

The Burāq The Earthly Mode Of Transportation

Then he brought the Burāq to me. It resembled lighting in swiftness and lustre, was of clear white colour, medium in size, smaller than a mule but bigger than a donkey, quick in movement that it put its feet on the farthest limit of the sight. He made me ride it and carried me to Jerusalem.

Masjid Al-Aqṣā

He tied the Burāq to the ring of that Mosque (Masjidul Aqṣā) to which all the Prophets in Jerusalem used to tie their animals. I led two Rak'ahs of prayer with the Prophets.

Al-Mi'raaj The Heavenly Mode Of Transportation

Then I was presented with Al-Mi'raaj, which is a being that looked like a ladder or a staircase, and I ascended to Heaven using the Mi'raaj.

Chapter 6
From Masjidul Ḥarām To Masjidul Aqṣā

The Details

The Holy Prophet Rasūlallāh ﷺ described this Miraculous Journey in many ḥadīth or Prophetic statements. The Journey from Makkah to Jerusalem is called the Israa', while the Journey from Masjidul Aqṣā to the Heavens and his meeting with Almighty Allāh ﷻ is called the Mi'raaj.

In The Home Of Umm Hāni

The Holy Prophet Muḥammad ﷺ said that he was one night sleeping at Makkah in the house of Umm Hāni, daughter of Abū Ṭālib and a sister of 'Alī, when Jibrīl ﷺ came to him.

Al-Haṭīm

The Angel Jibrīl ﷺ rent the roof of the house and brought the Prophet ﷺ to in Al-Ḥijr at the Ka'bah.[5] He opened my chest

5 Al-Ḥijr or Ḥijr Ismā'īl or Al-Ḥaṭīm is the semi-circular space under the waterspout

on the side of the heart, washed it with the water of Zamzam in a golden basin, filled it with wisdom and mercy, and put it back in its place.

Some additional details mentioned in the Ḥadith narrations include:

> Along with Angel Jibrīl ﷺ, there was Angel Mīkā'īl ﷺ. Another narration mentions a third angel.[6]
>
> He split the Prophet's ﷺ chest from his throat, on the side of his heart, to the bottom of his belly. Then Jibrīl ﷺ said to Mīkā'īl ﷺ: "Bring me a *Ṭast*[7] of water from Zamzam so that I may purify his heart and expand his breast."
>
> He took out his heart and washed it three times, removing from it all trace of harm[8] (مَا كَانَ بِهِ مِنْ أَذًى | *mā kāna bihi min adhā*).
>
> Angel Mīkā'īl went back and forth to him with the vessel of water from Zamzam three times.
>
> Then he brought him a golden vessel filled with wisdom and belief which he emptied into his chest. He filled his

(Mīzābur Raḥmah) which is open on both sides on the Northwest side of the Ka'bah.

6 The Angel Isrāfīl.

7 A vessel, usually made of copper.

8 Imām Taqiyyudīn As-Subkī said the "black clot" represents the potentiality of saytanic influence over every human heart, not its necessity, least of all in the case of the Prophet who is the Perfect Human and the Best of creation.

Imām Aḥmad Riḍā Khān said the "black clot" represents the part of the Prophet's ﷺ Mercy (Raḥmah) that would have benefited Shayṭān on Yawmul Qiyāmah.

chest with *Ḥilm*,[9] knowledge, certainty, and submission; then he closed it up. He sealed it between his shoulders with the seal of Prophethood.

The Burāq

Then he brought the Burāq, handsome-faced and bridled, a tall, white beast, bigger than the donkey but smaller than the mule. He could place his hooves at the farthest boundary of his gaze. He had long ears. Whenever he faced a mountain his hind legs would extend, and whenever he went downhill his front legs would extend. He had two wings on his thighs which lent strength to his legs.

He bucked when the Prophet ﷺ came to mount him. Jibrīl ﵇ put his hand on his mane and said: "Are you not ashamed, O Burāq? By Allāh, none has mounted you in all creation dearer to Allāh than he."

Hearing this, the Burāq was so ashamed that he sweated until he became soaked, and he stood still so that the Prophet ﷺ mounted him.

The other Prophets used to mount the Burāq before.
Sa'īd ibn al-Musayyib said: "It is the beast of Ibrāhīm ﵇ which he used to mount whenever he travelled to the Sacred House."

Al-Israa' & Jerusalem

Angel Jibrīl ﵇ departed with him. He placed himself on the right of the Burāq while Mīkā'īl was on his left.

9 *Ḥilm* (حِلْم)denotes intelligence, forbearance, gentleness, and good character.

(*In Imām Ibn Sa'ad's version:*) The one holding his stirrup was Jibrīl ﷺ and the one holding the reins of the Burāq was Mīkā'īl.

Ṭaybah - Madīnah

They travelled until they reached a land filled with date palms.
Angel Jibrīl ﷺ said to the Prophet ﷺ:

"Alight and pray here."

He did so and remounted, then Jibrīl ﷺ said:

"Do you know where you prayed?"

He ﷺ said no. Jibrīl ﷺ said:

"You prayed in *Ṭaybah* or land of pastures, and the Migration (Hijrah) will take place there.

Masjid Al-Umawi - Bilad Ash-Sham - Damascus - Syria

They travelled until they reached Bilad Ash-Sham.
Angel Jibrīl ﷺ said to the Prophet ﷺ:

"Alight and pray here."

He did so and remounted, then Jibrīl ﷺ said:

"Do you know where you prayed?"

He ﷺ said no. Jibrīl ﷺ said:

"You prayed in Masjid Al-Umawi. This is where 'Īsā Ibn Maryam will descend when he returns."

Madyan - The Tree Of Prophet Mūsā ﷺ

The Burāq continued his lightning flight, placing his hooves wherever his gaze could reach. Jibrīl ﷺ then said again:

"Alight and pray here."

He did so and remounted, then Jibrīl ﷺ said:

"Do you know where you prayed?"

He ﷺ said no. Jibrīl ﷺ said:

"You prayed in Madyan[10] at the tree of Mūsā."[11]

Mount Sinai - The Mount Of Sīnā'

The Burāq continued his lightning flight, then Jibrīl ﷺ said again:

"Alight and pray here."

He did so and remounted, then Jibrīl ﷺ said:

"Do you know where you prayed?"

He ﷺ said no. Jibrīl ﷺ said:

"You prayed at the Mountain of Sīnā' where Allāh addressed Mūsā."[12]

Bayt Laḥm - Bethlehem - Palestine

Then he reached a land where the palaces of Shām became visible to him. Jibrīl ﷺ said to him:

"Alight and pray."

He did so and remounted, then the Burāq continued his lightning Journey and Jibrīl ﷺ said:

"Do you know where you prayed?"

He ﷺ said no. Jibrīl ﷺ said:

"You prayed in Bayt Laḥm, where ʿĪsā Ibn Maryam was born."[13]

---

10 A city on the shore of the Red Sea bordering Tabūk near the valley of Shuʿayb.

11 The tree under which Prophet Mūsā ﷺ rested from fatigue and hunger during his flight from Firʿawn.

12 Mount Sinai in Palestine.

13 Bethlehem

A Devil From The Jinn

As the Prophet ﷺ was travelling mounted on the Burāq he saw a devil from the Jinn who was trying to get near him holding a firebrand. Everywhere the Prophet ﷺ turned he would see him. Jibrīl عليه السلام said to him:

> "Shall I teach you words which, if you say them, his firebrand will go out and he will fall dead?"

The Prophet ﷺ said:

> "Yes."

Jibrīl عليه السلام said: "Say:

أَعُوذُ بِوَجْهِ اللَّهِ الْكَرِيمِ
وبِكَلِمَاتِ اللَّهِ التَّامَّاتِ
اللَّاتِي لا يُجَاوِزُهُنَّ بَرٌّ وَلَا فَاجِرٌ
مِنْ شَرِّ ما يَنْزِلُ مِنَ السَّمَاءِ
وَمِنْ شَرِّ مَا يَعْرُجُ فِيهَا
وَمِنْ شَرِّ مَا ذَرَأَ فِي الأَرْضِ
وَمِنْ شَرِّ مَا يَخْرُجُ مِنْهَا
وَمِنْ شَرِّ فِتَنِ اللَّيْلِ والنَّهَارِ
ومِنْ شَرِّ طَوَارِقِ اللَّيْلِ والنَّهَارِ
إلاَّ طَارِقاً يَطْرُقُ بِخَيْرٍ يَا رَحْمٰنِ

A'ūdhu bi wajhillāhil karīm
Wa bi kalimātillāhit tāmmāt
al-lātī lā yujāwizuhunna bārrun wa lā fājir
min sharri mā yanzilu minas samā'
wa min sharri mā ya'ruju fīhā
wa min sharri mā dhara'a fil ard.
wa min sharri mā yakhruju minhā
wa min fitanil layli wan nahār
wa min ṭawāriqil layli wan nahār
illā ṭāriqin yaṭruqu bi khayrin Yā Raḥmān

I seek refuge in Allāh's Blessed Face
and in Allāh's perfect words
which neither the righteous nor the disobedient overstep
from evil that descends from the heaven
and evil that ascends to it
and evil that is created in the earth
and the trials of night and day
and the visitors of night and day
save the visitor that visits goodness upon us,
O Beneficent One!

At this the devil fell dead on his face and his firebrand went out.

The Mujāhidūn Those Who Strive In The Path Of Allāh ﷻ
They travelled until they reached a people who sowed in a day and reaped in a day. Every time they reaped, their harvest would be replenished as before. The Prophet ﷺ said:

"O Jibrīl! What is this?"

He replied:

> "These are the Mujāhidūn, those who strive in the path of Allāh the Exalted. Every good deed of theirs is multiplied for them seven hundred times, and whatever they spend returns multiplied."

The Pious Lady Who Combed The Hair Of Firʿawn's Daughter
The Prophet ﷺ then noticed a fragrant wind and said:

"O Jibrīl, what is this sweet scent?"

He (*Jibrīl*) replied:

> This is the scent of the lady who combed the hair of Firʿawn's[14] daughter and that of her children. As she combed the hair of Firʿawn's daughter the comb fell and she said: "Bismillāh taʾisa Firʿawn – In the name of Allāh, perish Firʿawn!" whereupon Firʿawn's daughter said: "Do you have a Lord other than my father?" She said yes. Firʿawn's daughter said: "Shall I tell my father?" She said yes. She told him and he summoned her and said: "Do you have a Lord other than me?" She replied: "Yes, my Lord and your Lord is Allāh."
>
> This woman had two sons and a husband. Firʿawn summoned them and he began to entice the woman and

14 Pharaoh.

her husband to give up their religion, but they refused. He said: “Then I shall have you killed.”

She said: “Please bury us all together in a single grave if you kill us.”
He replied: “Granted, and it is your right to ask us.”

He then ordered that a huge cow made of copper be filled with boiling liquid[15] and that she and her children be thrown into it.

The children were taken and thrown in one after the other. The second and youngest was still an infant at the breast. When they took him, he said: “Mother! fall and do not tarry for verily you are on the right.” Then she was thrown in with her children.

Ibn ʿAbbās ﷺ said: “Four spoke from the cradle as they were still infants: this child, Yūsuf’s witness,[16] Jurayj’s companion[17], and ʿĪsā ibn Maryam.”

15 Oil and Water.

16 Qur’ān, Sūrah Yūsuf, Chapter 12, Āyah 26: وَشَهِدَ شَاهِدٌ مِّنْ أَهْلِهَا (wa shahida shāhidun min ahlihā) – And one of her household saw (this) and bore witness.

17 The Ḥadīth is reported by Imām al-Bukhārī and Imām Muslim. Imām Ibn Ḥajar Al-ʿAsqalānī mentions that the account of the lady who combed the hair of Pharaoh’s daughter is narrated from Ibn ʿAbbās by Imāms Aḥmad, al-Ḥākim, Ibn Ḥibbān, and al-Bazzār. Imām Muslim in his *Ṣaḥīḥ*, Book of *Az-Zuhd wal Raqā’iq* (3005) mentions the part of the infant speaking to his mother before they are both thrown into the fire. The mention of Prophet Yūsuf’s witness in the verse: {وَشَهِدَ شَاهِدٌ مِّنْ أَهْلِهَا – And one of her household saw (this) and bore witness} (12:26) as being an infant is narrated from Ibn ʿAbbās by Ibn Abī Ḥātim with a weak chain, but is retained by Imām Ḥasan Al-Baṣrī and Saʿīd ibn Jubayr. It is also the explanation retained by Imām Suyūṭī and others in their commentaries of the Qur’ān. *Fatḥul Bārī* (1989 ed. 6:593-594).

Importance Of Performing Ṣalāh

Then the Prophet ﷺ saw some people whose heads were being shattered, then every time they would return to their original state and be shattered again without delay. He ﷺ said:

"O Jibrīl, who are these people?"

He (*Jibrīl*) replied:

"These are the people whose heads were too heavy [on their pillows] to get up and fulfil the obligatory prayers."

Consequence Of Not Paying Zakāt

Then he saw a people who wore loincloths on their fronts and on their backs. They were roaming the way camels and sheep roam about. They were eating thistles and Zaqqūm – the fruit of a tree that grows in hell and whose fruit resembles the heads of devils[18] – as well as white-hot coals and stones of Hell-Fire. He ﷺ said:

"Who are these, O Jibrīl?"

He (*Jibrīl*) replied:

"These are the ones who did not meet the obligation of paying alms from what they possessed, while Allāh never withheld anything from them."

Immorality

Then he saw a people who had in front of them excellent meats disposed in pots and also putrid meat, and they would eat from

18 Qur'ān, Sūrah Aṣ-Ṣāffāt, Chapter 37, Āyah 62-66:
أَذَٰلِكَ خَيْرٌ نُّزُلًا أَمْ شَجَرَةُ ٱلزَّقُّومِ ﴿٦٢﴾ إِنَّا جَعَلْنَـٰهَا فِتْنَةً لِّلظَّـٰلِمِينَ ﴿٦٣﴾ إِنَّهَا شَجَرَةٌ تَخْرُجُ فِىٓ أَصْلِ
ٱلْجَحِيمِ ﴿٦٤﴾ طَلْعُهَا كَأَنَّهُۥ رُءُوسُ ٱلشَّيَـٰطِينِ ﴿٦٥﴾ فَإِنَّهُمْ لَـَٔاكِلُونَ مِنْهَا فَمَالِـُٔونَ مِنْهَا ٱلْبُطُونَ ﴿٦٦﴾
{Is this better as a welcome, or the tree of Zaqqūm? Lo! We have appointed it a torment for wrong doers. Lo! it is a tree that springs in the heart of hell. Its crop is as it were the heads of devils. And lo! they verily must eat thereof, and fill (their) bellies therewith} (37:62-66).

the foul meat and not touch the good meat. He said:

"What is this, O Jibrīl?"

He (*Jibrīl*) replied:

"These are the men from your Community (Ummah) who had an excellent, lawful wife at home and who would go and see an infamous woman and spend the night with her; and the women who would leave her excellent, lawful husband to go and see an infamous man and spend the night with him."

People Who Obstruct The Path Of Others And Try To Harm Them

Then he came to a plank in the middle of the road which not even a piece of cloth nor less than that could cross except it would be pierced. He ﷺ said:

"What is this, O Jibrīl?"

He (*Jibrīl*) replied:

"This is what happens to those of your Community who sit in the middle of the road and harm passers-by"

and he recited:

وَلَا تَقْعُدُوا بِكُلِّ صِرَاطٍ تُوعِدُونَ وَتَصُدُّونَ عَن سَبِيلِ اللَّهِ مَنْ آمَنَ بِهِ وَتَبْغُونَهَا عِوَجًا...

{Lurk not on every road to threaten wayfarers and to turn away from the path of Allāh those who believe in Him, and to seek to make it (seem) crooked}

(Sūrah Al-Aʿrāf, 7:86)

Those Who Engage In Usury

The Prophet ﷺ saw a man swimming in a river of blood and he was being struck in his mouth with rocks which he then swallowed. The Prophet ﷺ asked:

> "What is this, O Jibrīl?"

He (*Jibrīl*) replied:

> "This is what happens to those who eat usury."

Betraying The Trust Of People

Then he saw a man who had gathered a stack of wood which he could not carry, yet he was adding more wood to it. He ﷺ said:

> "What is this, O Jibrīl?"

He (*Jibrīl*) replied:

> "This is a man from your Community who gets people's trusts when he cannot fulfil them, yet he insists on carrying them."

People Who Say What They Do Not Do

He then saw people whose tongues and lips were being sliced with metal knives. Every time they were sliced, they would return to their original state to be sliced again without respite. He ﷺ said:

> "Who are these, O Jibrīl?"

He (*Jibrīl*) replied:

> "These are the public speakers of division in your Community: they say what they do not do."

Backbiting – Eating The Flesh Of People

Then he passed by people who had copper nails with which they scratched their own faces and chests. He ﷺ asked:

"Who are these, O Jibrīl?"

He (*Jibrīl*) replied:

"These are the ones who ate the flesh of people and tarnished their reputations."

Consequence Of Telling An Enormity

Then he saw a small hole with a huge bull coming out of it. The bull began to try entering the hole again and was unable. The Prophet ﷺ said:

"What is this, O Jibrīl?"

He (*Jibrīl*) replied:

"This is the one in your Community who tells an enormity, then he feels remorse to have spoken it but is unable to take it back."

The Voice Of Paradise

Imām Ash-Shāmī [19]added: He (The Messenger of Allāh ﷺ) then came to a valley in which he breathed a sweet, cool breeze fragrant with musk and he heard a voice. He ﷺ said:

"What is this, O Jibrīl?"

He (*Jibrīl*) replied:

"This is the Voice of Paradise saying:

---

19 *Al-Ayāt al-'Aẓīmat al-Bāhira fī Mi'rāj Sayyid Ahlid Dunyā wal Ākhirah* ﷺ by the Ḥadīth Master Shamsuddīn Muḥammad ibn Yūsuf ibn 'Alī Ash-Shāmī Ad-Dimashqī Aṣ-Ṣāliḥī Ash-Shāfi'i Nazīl al-Qāhira (d. 942).
He is Imām Suyūṭī's student.

He is the author of a ten-volume biography of the Prophet ﷺ titled *Subul al-Hudā wal Rashād fī Sīrati Khayril 'Ibād* in which he compiled from over three hundred sources.

O my Lord, bring me what You have promised me!
Too abundant are my rooms, my gold-laced garments,
My silk, my brocades, my carpets, my pearls, my corals,
My silver, my gold, my goblets, my bowls, my pitchers,
My couches, my honey, my water, my milk, my wine!

And the Lord says:

You shall have every single Muslim man and woman,
Every believing man and woman,
Everyone who has believed in Me and My Messengers,
And did excellent deeds
Without associating a partner with Me,
Nor taking helpers besides Me!
Anyone who fears me shall be safe,
And whoever asks of Me, I shall give him,
And whoever loans[20] *Me something, I shall repay him,*
And whoever relies upon Me, I shall suffice him!
I am Allāh beside Whom there is no God.
I never fail in My promise.

قَدْ أَفْلَحَ ٱلْمُؤْمِنُونَ ١

{Successful indeed are the Believers}

(Sūratul Mu'minūn, 23:1)

... فَتَبَارَكَ ٱللَّهُ أَحْسَنُ ٱلْخَٰلِقِينَ ١٤

{So blessed be Allāh, the best of Creators!}

(Sūratul Mu'minūn, 23:14)

And Paradise answers:

"I accept."

20 Whoever spends their wealth in the way of Allāh, Allāh will repay them with more.

The Voice Of Hellfire

Then the Prophet ﷺ came to a valley in which he heard a detestable sound and smelled a foul wind. He ﷺ said:

"What is this, O Jibrīl?"

He (*Jibrīl*) replied:

"This is the sound of Hellfire saying:

O Lord, give me what You promised me!
Abundant are my chains, my yokes, my punishments,
My fires, my thistles, my pus, my tortures!
My depth is abysmal, my heat unbearable!
Therefore, give me what You promised me!

And the Lord replies:

You shall have every idolater and idolatress,
Every disbelieving man and woman, every foul one,
And every tyrant who does not believe
in the Day of Reckoning!

The Anti-Christ – Ad-Dajjāl

The Prophet ﷺ saw the Anti-Christ (Ad-Dajjāl) in his actual likeness. He saw him with his own eyes, not in a dream. It was said to him ﷺ:

"O Messenger of Allāh, how was he when you saw him?"

He ﷺ replied:

"Mammoth-sized (faylamāniyyan), extremely pale and white (aqmaru hijān), and one of his eyes is protuberant as if it were a twinkling star.

His hair is like the branches of a tree. He resembles 'Abdul 'Uzzā Ibn Qaṭṭān."[21]

The Column Of Islam

The Prophet ﷺ saw a pearl-like white column which the angels were carrying. He ﷺ said:

"What is this you are carrying?"

They replied:

"The Column of Islam. We have been ordered to place it in Ash-Shām."

The Herald Of The Jews

As the Prophet ﷺ was travelling he heard someone calling him from his right:

"Muḥammad! Look at me, I want to ask you something!" But the Prophet ﷺ did not respond.

Then he ﷺ said:

"Who was this, O Jibrīl?"

He (*Jibrīl*) replied:

"This is the herald of the Jews. If you had answered him your Community (Ummah) would have followed Judaism."

The Herald Of The Christians

The Prophet ﷺ continued travelling and he heard someone calling him from his left:

"Muḥammad! Look at me, I want to ask you something!" But the Prophet ﷺ did not respond.

21 'Abdul 'Uzzā Ibn Qaṭṭān died in Jahiliyyah, in the Time of Ignorance.

Then he ﷺ said:

"Who was this, O Jibrīl?"

He (*Jibrīl*) replied:

"This is the herald of the Christians. If you had answered him, your Community would have followed Christianity."

The Temptation Of The Dunya

The Prophet ﷺ continued travelling and passed by a woman with bare arms, decked with every female ornament Allāh had created. She said:

"Muḥammad! Look at me, I need to ask you something." But he did not look at her.

Then he ﷺ said:

"Who was this, O Jibrīl?"

He (*Jibrīl*) replied:

"This was the world (Dunyā). If you had answered her, your Community would have preferred this World (Dunya) to the Hereafter (Ākhirah)."

Iblīs – Shayṭān – The Enemy Of Allāh ﷻ

As the Prophet ﷺ travelled on, he passed by an old man who was some distance away from his path saying:

"Come hither, O Muḥammad!"

But Jibrīl ﷺ said:

"Nay! Go on, O Muḥammad!"

The Prophet ﷺ went on and then said:

"Who was this, O Jibrīl?" He replied: "This was Allāh's enemy, Iblīs. He wanted you to incline towards him."

The Remaining Time Of The Dunya

He went on and passed by an old woman on the roadside who said:

> "O Muḥammad! Look at me, I need to ask you something!"
> But he did not look at her.

Then he ﷺ said:

> "Who was this, O Jibrīl?"

He (*Jibrīl*) replied:

> "The world has as much left to live as the remaining lifetime of this old woman."

Other Prophets Greeting The Holy Prophet Muḥammad ﷺ

Imām Ash-Shāmī[22] added: As the Holy Prophet ﷺ continued his Journey, he was met by some of Allāh's ﷻ creatures who said:

> "Peace be upon you, O First One! (Yā Awwal).
> Peace upon you, O Last One! (Yā Ākhir).
> Peace be upon you, O Gatherer! (Yā Ḥāshir)."

Angel Jibrīl ﷷ said to him:

> "Return their greeting," and he ﷺ did.

Then he ﷺ saw them another time and they said the same thing.
Then he ﷺ saw them a third time and again they greeted him.
The Holy Prophet ﷺ said:

> "Who are they, O Jibrīl?"

He (*Jibrīl*) replied:

> "Ibrāhīm, Mūsā, and 'Īsā."

---

22 *Al-Ayāt al-'Aẓīmat al-Bāhira fī Mi'rāj Sayyid Ahlid Dunyā wal Ākhirah* ﷺ by the Ḥadīth Master Shamsuddīn Muḥammad ibn Yūsuf ibn 'Alī Ash-Shāmī Ad-Dimashqī As-Ṣāliḥī Ash-Shāfi'i Nazīl al-Qāhira (d. 942).

Greetings Of Prophet Mūsā ﷺ

The Prophet ﷺ then passed by Mūsā ﷺ as he was praying in his grave at a place of red sandhills. He was tall, with long hair and brown complexion, similar to one of the Shanū'a – the [Yemeni] men of pure lineage and manly virtue.

He (*Mūsā*) was saying with a loud voice:

"You have honoured him and preferred him!"

Then the Prophet ﷺ greeted him and he returned his greeting. Mūsā ﷺ said:

"Who is this with you, O Jibrīl?"

He (*Jibrīl*) replied:

"This is Aḥmad ."

He (*Mūsā*) said:

"Welcome to the Arabian Prophet who acted perfectly with his Community!" And Mūsā made an invocation for blessing on his behalf.

Then he (*Mūsā*) said:

"Ask ease for your Community."

They continued travelling and the Prophet ﷺ said:

"O Jibrīl! Who was this?"

He (*Jibrīl*) replied:

"This was Mūsā Ibn 'Imrān."

The Prophet ﷺ asked:

"Who was he reprimanding?"

He (*Jibrīl*) said:

"He was reprimanding his Lord."

The Prophet ﷺ said:

"He reprimands (his Lord) and raises his voice against his Lord??"

Jibrīl ﷺ said:

"Allāh the Exalted well knows Mūsā's bluntness."

Du'ā' of Prophet Ibrāhīm ﷺ

He passed by a large tree whose fruit seemed like a thornless berry (of the kind that gives shade to men and cattle). Under it an old man was resting with his dependents. There were lamps and a great light could be seen. The Prophet ﷺ said:

"Who is this, O Jibrīl?"

He (*Jibrīl*) replied:

"Your father, Ibrāhīm."

The Prophet ﷺ greeted him and Ibrāhīm ﷺ returned his greeting and said:

"Who is this with you, O Jibrīl?"

He (*Jibrīl*) replied:

"This is your son Aḥmad."

Prophet Ibrāhīm ﷺ said:

> "Welcome to the unlettered Arabian Prophet who has conveyed the message of his Lord and acted with perfect sincerity with his Community!
>
> O my son, you are going to meet your Lord tonight, and your Community is the last and weakest of all Communities – therefore, if you are able to have your need fulfilled concerning your Community, or most of it, be sure to do it!"

Then he invoked for goodness on the Prophet Muḥammad's ﷺ behalf.

Hellfire Looked Like Cinders

They continued travelling until they reached the valley that is in the city – that is: the Hallowed House [Jerusalem] – when lo and behold! Hell-Fire was shown to them like a carpet unfolded. They [the Companions] said:

"O Messenger of Allāh! What did it look like?"

He ﷺ replied:

"Like cinders."

Arrival at Jerusalem – The Hallowed City

He continued travelling until he reached the city of the Hallowed House and he entered it by its southern gate. He dismounted the Burāq and tied it at the gate of the mosque, using the ring by which the Prophets tied it before him.

One narration states that Angel Jibrīl ﷺ came to the rock and placed his fingers in it, piercing it, then he tied the Burāq using the spot he had hollowed out.

Chapter 7
Events at Masjidul Aqṣā

The Details

The Noble Prophet's Entrance to Masjidul Aqṣā[23]
The Holy Prophet, Rasūlallāh ﷺ, continued travelling until he reached the city of the Hallowed House and he entered it by its southern gate.

He ﷺ dismounted the Burāq and tied it at the gate of the mosque, using the ring by which the Prophets tied it before him.

One narration states that Angel Jibrīl ﷺ came to the Rock and placed his fingers in it, piercing it, then he tied the Burāq using the spot he had hollowed out.

The Prophet ﷺ entered the Mosque from a gate through which

23 The Noble Scholar, His Eminence Shaykh Muḥammad Ibn 'Alawi Ibn 'Abbās Ibn 'Abdul 'Aziz Al-Mālikī Al-Ḥasanī Al-Makkī, Shaykhul Islam fil Baladil Ḥarām. The title of his book is: *Al-Anwār al-Bahiyyah min Isrā' wa Mi'rāj Khayril Bariyyah*, "The Resplendent Lights of the Night-Journey and Ascension of the Best of Creation," (Makkah, 1414/1993). Translated by Shaykh Gibril Fouad Haddad.

the sun and the moon could be seen when they set.

He ﷺ prayed two cycles of prayer and did not tarry long before a large throng of people had gathered.

The Prophet ﷺ recognized all the Prophets, some standing in prayer, some bowing, some prostrating.

Then Angel Jibrīl ﷺ called the Adhān for the Prayer and the final call to Prayer (Iqāmah) was made.

They rose and stood in lines, waiting for the one who would lead them. Jibrīl ﷺ took the hand of the Prophet ﷺ and brought him forward. He ﷺ led them in two cycles of Prayer.[24]

The following is related from Sayyidunā Ka'ab ﷺ:

> The Angel Jibrīl ﷺ raised the call to prayer. The angels descended from the heavens. Almighty Allāh ﷻ gathered all the Messengers and Prophets. Then the Prophet ﷺ prayed as the leader of the angels and Messengers. Jibrīl ﷺ told the Prophet ﷺ:
>
> > *"Every single Prophet whom Allāh has ever sent prayed behind you."*

Imām Ash-Shāmī adds: Abū Hurayrah's narration related by

24 The Noble Scholar, Shaykh Muḥammad ibn 'Alawī Al-Mālikī said that this took place before his ascension according to the highest probability, quoting Imām Najmuddīn Al-Ghayṭī who said: "The narrations agree to the fact that the Prophet ﷺ prayed among the other Prophets in Jerusalem before his ascension."
Imām Al-Qāḍī 'Iyāḍ mentioned this possibility as well.
Imām Ibn Ḥajar Al-'Asqalānī said: "This is apparently the case.
Imām Ibn Kathīr also declared this scenario to be the sound one.

Al-Ḥākim who declared it sound, and by Al-Bayhaqī, states that the Prophet ﷺ met all the Prophets.

Prophet Ibrāhīm ﷺ glorified his Lord and said:[25]

> "Praise be to Allāh Who has taken me as His intimate friend, Who has given me an immense kingdom, Who has made me a prayerful Community and one by whom prayer is led, Who has rescued me from the fire and made it cool and safe for me!"

Then Prophet Mūsā ﷺ glorified his Lord and said:

> "Praise be to Allāh Who has spoken to me directly, Who has brought to pass the destruction of Fir'awn and the salvation of the Children of Israel at my hands, and Who has made from among my Community a people who guide others through truth and establish justice upon it!"

Then Prophet Dāwūd ﷺ glorified his Lord and said:

> "Praise be to Allāh Who has brought me an immense kingdom, Who has softened iron for my hands and subjected to me the mountains and the birds which laud Him, and has given me wisdom and unmistakable judgement in my speech!"

Then Prophet Sulaymān ﷺ glorified his Lord and said:

> "Praise be to Allāh Who has subjected the winds to my

25 Imām Ash-Shāmī: *Al-Ayāt al-'Aẓīmat al-Bāhira fī Mi'rāj Sayyid Ahlid Dunyā wal Ākhirah* ﷺ by the Ḥadīth Master Shamsuddīn Muḥammad ibn Yūsuf ibn 'Alī Ash-Shāmī Ad-Dimashqī As-Ṣāliḥī Ash-Shāfi'i Nazīl al-Qāhira (d. 942).
He is Imām Suyūṭī's student. He is the author of a ten-volume biography of the Prophet ﷺ titled *Subul al-Hudā wal Rashād fī Sīrati Khayril 'Ibād* in which he compiled from over three hundred sources.

> command as well as the Jinns, so that they did as I wished and constructed for me elevated sanctuaries, images, large bowls the size of ponds, and vessels fixed in their spot [due to their size]! Who has taught me the language of birds and has brought me a portion of every good thing! Who has subjected to me the armies of the Jinns and the birds and has preferred me over many of His believing servants! Who has brought me an immense kingdom which no one after me may possess! And Who has made my kingdom a goodly one wherein there is no reckoning nor punishment!"

Then Prophet 'Īsā Ibn Maryam ﷺ glorified his Lord and said:

> "Praise be to Allāh Who has made me His Word! Who has fashioned me after Ādam's likeness whom He created out of earth then said to him: Be! and he was. Who has taught me the Book and the Wisdom and the Torāh and the Injīl! Who has caused me to heal the blind and the leper and to raise the dead by Allāh's permission! Who has raised me and cleansed me and granted me and my mother protection against the cursed devil, so that the devil had no path by which to harm us! (End of Imām Ash-Shāmī's addition)."

Every Prophet then glorified his Lord in the best language that they could speak. Then the Holy Prophet, Rasūlallāh ﷺ said:[26]

> "All of you have glorified their Lord and I am going to glorify Him also:

---

26 Imām Najmuddīn Al-Ghayṭī: *Al-Ibtihāj fil-Kalām 'alal-Isrā' wal Mi'rāj* by the Ḥadith scholar Najmuddīn Abul Mawāhib Muḥammad ibn Aḥmad ibn 'Alī ibn Abī Bakr Al-Ghayṭī As-Sakandarī al-Miṣrī al-Shāfi'ī (d. 981). See Imām Al-Kattānī, *al-Risāla al-Mustaṭrafa*. Imām Najmuddīn Al-Ghayṭī's work was published under the title *Mawsū'at al-Isrā' wal Mi'rāj al-Mūsāmmāt Taṭrīz ad-Dībāj bi-Ḥaqā'iq al-Isrā' wal Mi'rāj* (Beirut: Dār wa Maktabat al-Hilāl, 1994).

الْحَمْدُ لِلَّهِ الَّذِي أَرْسَلَنِي رَحْمَةً لِلْعَالَمِينَ وَكَافَّةً لِلنَّاسِ بَشِيرًا وَنَذِيرًا ،
وَأَنْزَلَ عَلَيَّ الْقُرْءَانَ فِيهِ تِبْيَانٌ لِكُلِّ شَيْءٍ ، وَجَعَلَ أُمَّتِي خَيْرَ أُمَّةٍ
أُخْرِجَتْ لِلنَّاسِ ، وَجَعَلَ أُمَّتِي أُمَّةً وَسَطًا ، وَجَعَلَ أُمَّتِي هُمُ الْأَوَّلِينَ
وَهُمُ الْآخِرِينَ ، وَشَرَحَ لِي صَدْرِي ، وَوَضَعَ عَنِّي وِزْرِي وَرَفَعَ لِي
ذِكْرِي ، وَجَعَلَنِي فَاتِحًا وَخَاتَمًا

Al-ḥamdu lillāhil ladhī arsalanī raḥmatan lil-ʻālamīn
Wa kāffatan lin-nāsi bashīran wa-nadhīrā
Wa anzala ʿalayyal qur'āna fīhi tibyānun li kulli shay'in
Wa jaʿala ummatī khayra ummatin ukhrijat lin-nās
Wa jaʿala ummatī ummatan wasaṭā
Wa jaʿala ummatī humul awwalīna wa humul ākhirīn
Wa sharaḥa lī ṣadrī wa waḍaʿa ʿannī wazrī
Wa rafaʿa lī dhikrī
Wa jaʿalanī fātiḥan khātiman!

Praise to Allāh Who has sent me as a mercy to the worlds,
Sent to all without exception,
A bearer of glad tidings and a warner!
Who has caused to descend upon me the Qur'ān
In which there is a perfect exposition of all things!
Who has made my Community (Ummah) the best Community ever brought out for the benefit of mankind!
Who has made my Community (Ummah) a median and a middle Nation!
Who has made my Community, in truth,
The first [in Paradise] and the last [in creation] of all Communities!
Who has expanded my breast

And relieved me of my burden!
Who has exalted (and raised up) my name,
And made me the Opener and the Sealer!

Upon hearing this, Angel Jibrīl ﷺ said:

"In this has Muḥammad ﷺ bested you!"

Then they evoked the matter of the Hour and referred it to Prophet Ibrāhīm ﷺ, but he said:

"I have no knowledge of it."

They turned to Prophet Mūsā ﷺ but he said:

"I have no knowledge of it."

They turned to Prophet 'Īsā ﷺ and he said:

"As for the time when it shall befall, no one knows it except Allāh. But this is what my Lord has assured me [concerning what precedes it]. The Dajjāl or Anti-Christ shall come forth and I will face him with two rods. At my sight he shall melt like lead. Allāh shall cause his destruction as soon as he sees me. It will be so that the very stones will say: *"O Muslim, behind me hides a disbeliever, therefore come and kill him!"* And Allāh shall cause them all to die.

People shall then return to their countries and nations. At that time Ya'jūj and Ma'jūj [Gog and Magog] shall come out. They shall come from every direction. They shall trample all nations underfoot. Whatever they come upon, they shall destroy.

They shall drink up every body of water. At long last the people shall come to me bewailing about them. At that time, I will invoke Allāh against them so that He will destroy them and cause their death until the whole earth will reek of their stench. Allāh will then send down rain which shall carry their bodies away and hurl them into the sea.

I have been assured by my Lord that once all this takes place then the Hour will be as the pregnant mother at the last stages of her pregnancy. Her family does not know when she shall suddenly give birth – by night or by day."

Vessels of Choice: Milk, Wine, Water, Honey

The Prophet ﷺ then felt the greatest thirst that he had ever felt, whereupon Jibrīl ﷺ brought him a vessel of wine and a vessel of milk. He chose the milk.

Jibrīl ﷺ said:

> "You have chosen Fiṭrah – natural disposition.
> Had you chosen to drink the wine, your Community would have strayed from the right way and none but a few of them would have followed you."[27]

Another narration states: There were three vessels and the third contained water. Jibrīl ﷺ said:

> "If you had drunk the water your Community would have perished by drowning."

Another narration states that one of the vessels presented to him

27 The Prophet ﷺ said: "Every child is born with natural disposition (*kullu mawlūdin yūladu 'alal Fiṭrah*). Then his parents convert him to Judaism, or Christianity, or Zoroastrianism. It is the same with the animal which delivers a fully formed (*jam'ā'*) calf. Do you find that it is missing part of its facial features (*jad'ā'*)?" Narrated from Abū Hurayrah by Imām Al-Bukhārī, Imām Muslim, Imām Abū Dāwūd, Imām Aḥmad, and Imām Mālik. Imām Al-Tirmidhī also narrates it (ḥasan ṣaḥīḥ) but omits the mention of the animal and narrates the addition: "O Messenger of Allāh, what if the child dies before that?" He replied: "Allāh knows best what they would have done."

contained honey instead of water.

The Holy Prophet ﷺ chose the Vessel containing Milk.

The Ḥouris – Maidens of Paradise

The Prophet ﷺ then saw the wide-eyed maidens of Paradise at the left of the Rock. He greeted them and they returned his greeting. Then he asked them something and they replied with an answer that cools the eyes.

The Mi'raaj – The Second Mode of Transportation[28]

Then the Prophet ﷺ was brought the ladder by which the spirits of the children of Ādam ﷺ ascend. Creation never saw a more beautiful object. It had alternate stairs of silver and gold and came down from the Highest and Amplest Garden of Paradise, Jannat al- Firdaws. It was encrusted with pearls and surrounded with angels on its right and left.

28 The Noble Scholar, His Eminence Shaykh Muḥammad Ibn 'Alawi Ibn 'Abbās Ibn 'Abdul 'Aziz Al-Mālikī Al-Ḥasanī Al-Makkī, Shaykhul Islam fil Baladil Ḥarām. The title of his book is: *Al-Anwār al-Bahiyyah min Isrā' wa Mi'rāj Khayril Bariyyah*, "The Resplendent Lights of the Night-Journey and Ascension of the Best of Creation," (Makkah, 1414/1993). Translated by Shaykh Gibril Fouad Haddad.

PART FOUR

MIʿRAAJUN NABI: THE PROPHETIC HEAVENLY ASCENSION

Chapter 8

Miʿraajun Nabi

The Events as Narrated in the Original Sources

Al-Miʿraaj The Heavenly Mode Of Transportation

Then I was presented with Al-Miʿraaj, which is a being that looked like a ladder or a staircase, and I ascended to Heaven using the Miʿraaj.

First Heaven

When I reached the First Heaven, the guarding angel said: "Blessed be thy arrival" and opened the door of the heaven. The angels congratulated me and opened the gate."

The Prophet ﷺ spoke to Adam عليه السلام in the first heaven. He found him in the company of the souls of the dead, divided into two groups, good and bad.

Second Heaven

The Prophet ﷺ continued: "In the second heaven, I visited 'Īsā (Jesus) and Yaḥyā (John the Baptist), (Peace be upon them) ﵉, and saluted them. They returned my salutation and said: "Good brother, blessed be thy arrival!" Then they expressed their faith in my prophethood.

Third Heaven

Then I reached the third heaven and met Yūsuf (Joseph), (Peace be upon him) ﵇, and saluted him. Joseph looked like a full moon in the striking radiance of his beauty. He welcomed me and returned my salutation and expressed his faith in my prophethood.

Fourth Heaven

Then I was carried to the fourth heaven where I met Prophet Idrīs (Enoch).

Fifth Heaven

Then I was carried to the fifth heaven. There I met Prophet Hārūn (Aaron), the handsomest old man I ever saw, with silver white hair, and a long, white beard. I saluted him and he returned my salutation and expressed his faith in my prophethood.

Sixth Heaven

Then I reached the sixth heaven. I met Prophet Mūsā (Moses) ﵇ there. I saluted him and he returned my salutation.

Seventh Heaven

Then I reached the seventh heaven and met Prophet Ibrāhīm (Abraham) and saluted him.

Al-Baytul Maʿmūr

I was shown Al-Baytul Maʿmūr which is a Kaʿbah in heaven encompassed daily by seventy thousand angels, so that the angels who once performed Ṭawāf around it will not get a second opportunity to do so.

Heaven And Hell

I was shown paradise and hell.

Sidratul Muntahā

Then I was taken to Al-Sidratul Muntahā.

In The Presence Of Almighty Allāh ﷻ

Jibrīl ﷺ stopped there and I went on to be presented to the Divine presence. I experienced the thrill of witnessing the Divine Glory and Manifestation.

The Command To Perform Ṣalāh

Fifty daily prayers were ordained for my followers. On my return I spoke to Moses ﷺ and told him that my followers had been enjoined to pray fifty times a day.

Moses ﷺ said:

> "Your followers cannot perform so many prayers. I have already tried the children of Israel. Go back to Allāh and ask for a remission in number."

I went back to the presence of Allāh and stated that my followers could not bear the burden of so many prayers. Almighty Allāh, Glory be to Him, made a reduction to forty prayers.

When I reported this to Moses ﷺ, he urged me again to request for a further reduction. I again begged my Lord to reduce the number still further.

I went again and again in the presence of Allāh at the suggestion of Moses ﷺ for reduction in the number until these were reduced to five only.

Moses again asked me to implore for further reduction, but I said:

> "I feel ashamed now of repeatedly asking Allāh for further reduction. I accept the five daily prayers. Allāh has commanded that these five prayers shall be rewarded as fifty prayers."

Chapter 9

The Prophetic Heavenly Ascension

The Details

Journey Through The Seven Heavens

The Miʿraaj – The Heavenly Mode of Transportation

The Holy Prophet Rasūlallāh ﷺ was brought the Miʿraaj which the spirits of the children of Ādam عليه السلام ascend. Creation never saw a more beautiful object.

It had alternate stairs of silver and gold and came down from the Highest and Amplest Garden of Paradise, Jannat al- Firdaws. It was encrusted with pearls and surrounded with angels on its right and left. The Miʿraaj was the Second Mode of Transportation for this Miraculous Journey. The first one was the Burāq.

The First Heaven[29]

The Prophet ﷺ began his ascent with Angel Jibrīl ﷺ until they reached one of the gates of the First (nearest) Heaven called Bābul Ḥafaẓah.

There an angel stood guard, named Ismāʿīl ﷺ, who is the custodian of the First Heaven. He inhabits the wind. He never ascended to the heaven nor descended to earth except on the day that the Prophet ﷺ died, blessings and peace upon him.

In front of him stood seventy thousand angels, each angel commanding an army of seventy thousand more.

Jibrīl ﷺ asked for the gate to be opened. Someone said:
"Who is this?"
"Jibrīl."
"Who is with you?
"Muḥammad."
"Has he been sent for?"
"Yes."
"Welcome to him, from his family! May Allāh grant him long life! A brother and deputy, and what an excellent brother and deputy! What an excellent visit this is!"

The gate of the First Heaven was opened. When they came in, they saw Ādam ﷺ the father of humanity, just as he was on the very day

29 The Noble Scholar, His Eminence Shaykh Muḥammad Ibn 'Alawi Ibn 'Abbās Ibn 'Abdul 'Aziz Al-Mālikī Al-Ḥasanī Al-Makkī, Shaykhul Islam fil Baladil Ḥarām. The title of his book is: *Al-Anwār al-Bahiyyah min Isrā' wa Mi'rāj Khayril Bariyyah*, "The Resplendent Lights of the Night-Journey and Ascension of the Best of Creation," (Makkah, 1414/1993). Translated by Shaykh Gibril Fouad Haddad.

Almighty Allāh ﷻ created him in his complete form.[30]
The spirits of the Prophets and of Ādam's ﷺ other faithful offsprings were being shown to him, whereupon he would say:

> "A goodly spirit and a goodly soul, put it in the Highest ('illiyyīn)!"[31]

Then the spirits of Ādam's ﷺ disbelieving offsprings were shown to him and he would say:

> "A foul spirit and a foul soul, put it in the lowest layer of Hell (Sijjīn)!"[32]

The Prophet ﷺ saw on Ādam's right great dark masses and a gate exuding a fragrant smell, and on his left great dark masses and a gate exuding a foul, putrid smell.

Whenever Ādam ﷺ looked to his right he would smile and be happy, and whenever he looked to his left he would be sad and weep.

The Prophet ﷺ greeted him and Ādam returned his greeting and said:

> "Welcome to the righteous son and the righteous Prophet!"

The Prophet ﷺ said:

> "What is this, O Jibrīl?"

He (*Jibrīl*) replied:

> "This is your father Ādam ﷺ and the dark throngs are the souls of his children. Those on the right are the people of

30 That is, without passing him through the stages of embryonic formation. The scholars have explained in this sense the Ḥadīth "Allāh created Ādam in his form," narrated by Abū Hurayrah and reported by Imām Bukhārī and Imām Muslim, i.e. in his finished form.

31 Illiyyīn - The place where the Believing Souls are kept.

32 Sijjīn - The Place where Disbelieving Souls are kept.

> Paradise and those on the left are the people of the Fire. Whenever he looks to his right he smiles and is glad, and whenever he looks to his left, he is sad and weeps. The door to his right is the gate of Paradise. Whenever he sees those of his offspring enter it he smiles happily. The door to his left is the gate of Hellfire. Whenever he sees those of his offspring enter it he weeps sadly."

Imām Ash-Shāmī added:[33] Then the Prophet ﷺ continued for a little while. He saw a table spread in which there were pieces of good meat which no one approached, and another table spread in which were pieces of rotten meat which stank, surrounded by people who were eating it. The Prophet ﷺ asked:

> "O Jibrīl, who are these?"

He (*Jibrīl*) replied:

> "These are those of your Community (Ummah) who abandon what is lawful and proceed to what is unlawful."

Then the Prophet ﷺ went on for a little while. He saw groups of people whose lips resembled the lips of camels. Their mouths were being pried open and they would be stoned.

One version says: A rock from Hellfire was placed in their mouths and then it would come out again from their posteriors. The Prophet ﷺ said:

> "I heard them clamouring to Allāh."

---

33 Imām Ash-Shāmī: *Al-Ayāt al-'Aẓīmat al-Bāhira fī Mi'rāj Sayyid Ahlid Dunyā wal Ākhirah* ﷺ by the Ḥadīth Master Shamsuddīn Muḥammad ibn Yūsuf ibn 'Alī Ash-Shāmī Ad-Dimashqī As-Ṣāliḥī Ash-Shāfi'i Nazīl al-Qāhira (d. 942).
He is Imām Suyūṭī's student. He is the author of a ten-volume biography of the Prophet ﷺ titled *Subul al-Hudā wal Rashād fī Sīrati Khayril 'Ibād* in which he compiled from over three hundred sources.

He ﷺ asked:

> "O Jibrīl, who are these?"

He (*Jibrīl*) replied:

> "They are those of your Community who eat up the property of orphans and commit injustice. They are eating nothing but a fire for their bellies, and they shall be roasted in it."

Then the Prophet ﷺ went on for a little while. He saw women suspended by their breasts and others hanging upside down. The Prophet ﷺ said:

> "I heard them clamouring to Allāh."

He ﷺ asked:

> "Who are these, O Jibrīl?"

He (*Jibrīl*) replied:

> "These are the women who commit fornication and then kill their children."

The Severe Consequences of Backbiting

Then the Prophet ﷺ went on for a little while. He saw groups of people whose sides were being cut off for meat and they were being devoured. They were being told:

> "Eat, just as you used to eat the flesh of your brother."

The Prophet ﷺ said:

> "O Jibrīl, who are these?"

He (*Jibrīl*) replied:

> "They are the slanderers of your Community who bring shame to others."

Then the Prophet ﷺ continued for a little while, and he found the consumers of usury and of the property of orphans, the fornicators and adulterers, and others, in various horrible states like those that have been described or worse.

The Second Heaven[34]

Then they ascended to the Second Heaven. Jibrīl ﷺ asked for the gate to be opened. Someone said:

"Who is this?"

"Jibrīl."

"Who is with you?

"Muḥammad."

"Has he been sent for?"

"Yes."

"Welcome to him, from his family! May Allāh grant him long life, a brother and deputy, and what excellent brother and deputy! What an excellent visit this is!"

The gate was opened. When they came in they saw the sons of the two sisters: ʿĪsā Ibn Maryam ﷺ and Yaḥyā Ibn Zakariyyā.

They resembled each other in clothing and hair. Each had with him a large company of his people. ʿĪsā was curly-haired, of medium build, leaning towards fair complexion, with hair let down as if he were coming out of the bath. He resembled ʿUrwā ibn Masʿūd al-Thaqafī.[35]

---

34 Imām Najmuddīn Al-Ghayṭī: *Al-Ibtihāj fil-Kalām ʿalal-Isrāʾ wal Miʿrāj* by the Ḥadith scholar Najmuddīn Abul Mawāhib Muḥammad ibn Aḥmad ibn ʿAlī ibn Abī Bakr Al-Ghayṭī As-Sakandarī al-Miṣrī al-Shāfiʿī (d. 981).

See Imām Al-Kattānī, *al-Risāla al-Mustaṭrafa.* Imām Najmuddīn Al-Ghayṭī's work was published under the title *Mawsūʿat al-Isrāʾ wal Miʿrāj al-Mūsāmmāt Taṭrīz ad-Dībāj bi-Ḥaqāʾiq al-Isrāʾ wal Miʿrāj* (Beirut: Dār wa Maktabat al-Hilāl, 1994).

35 The Companion ʿUrwā Ibn Masʿūd al-Thaqafī [R.A.] was one of the dignitaries of

The Prophet ﷺ greeted them and they returned his greeting. Then they said:

> "Welcome to the righteous brother and the righteous Prophet!"

Then they invoked for goodness on his behalf.

The Third Heaven[36]

After this the Prophet ﷺ and Angel Jibrīl ؑ ascended to the Third Heaven. Sayyidunā Jibrīl ؑ asked for the gate to be opened. Someone said:

"Who is this?"

> "Jibrīl."

"Who is with you?

> "Muḥammad."

"Has he been sent for?"

> "Yes."

"Welcome to him, from his family! May Allāh grant him long life, a brother and deputy, and what excellent brother and deputy! What an excellent visit this is!"

The gate was opened. When they came in they saw Prophet Yūsuf ؑ, and with him stood a large company of his people. The Prophet ﷺ greeted him and he returned his greeting and said: "Welcome

---

the town of Ṭā'if. Imām Ibn Ḥajar in *al-Iṣābah* (4:492-493) and Imām Ibn 'Abdul Barr in *al-Istī'āb* (8:1066-1067) relate that he alone responded to the Prophet's ﷺ invitation to that city by following him and declaring his acceptance of Islam. Then he asked for permission to return to his people and speak to them.

36 The Noble Scholar, His Eminence Shaykh Muḥammad Ibn 'Alawi Ibn 'Abbās Ibn 'Abdul 'Aziz Al-Mālikī Al-Ḥasanī Al-Makkī, Shaykhul Islam fil Baladil Ḥarām. The title of his book is: *Al-Anwār al-Bahiyyah min Isrā' wa Mi'rāj Khayril Bariyyah*, "The Resplendent Lights of the Night-Journey and Ascension of the Best of Creation," (Makkah, 1414/1993). Translated by Shaykh Gibril Fouad Haddad.

to the righteous brother and the righteous Prophet!" Then he invoked for goodness on his behalf.

Yūsuf had been granted the gift of beauty. One narration states: He was the most handsome creation that Allāh had ever created and he surpassed people in beauty the way the full moon surpasses all other stars. The Prophet asked:

"Who is this, O Jibrīl?"

He (*Jibrīl*) replied:

"Your brother Yūsuf."

Imām Busayri mentioned that only the Holy Prophet Rasūlallāh was more handsome and more beautiful than Prophet Yūsuf. The women in the court of the 'Azīz of Egypt, when they saw the beauty of Prophet Yūsuf, they cut their hands. But if they had seen the true Beauty of the Messenger of Allāh Rasūlallāh, they would have cut their necks!

For the Holy Prophet is The Best of All Creation (خَيْرُ خَلْقِ اَللَّهِ – *Khayru Khalqil-lāh*).

The Fourth Heaven[37]

Then they ascended to the Fourth Heaven. Jibrīl asked for the gate to be opened. Someone said:

"Who is this?"

---

37 Imām Ash-Shāmī: *Al-Ayāt al-'Aẓīmat al-Bāhira fī Mi'rāj Sayyid Ahlid Dunyā wal Ākhirah* by the Ḥadīth Master Shamsuddīn Muḥammad ibn Yūsuf ibn 'Alī Ash-Shāmī Ad-Dimashqī As-Ṣāliḥī Ash-Shāfi'i Nazīl al-Qāhira (d. 942).
He is Imām Suyūṭī's student. He is the author of a ten-volume biography of the Prophet titled *Subul al-Hudā wal Rashād fī Sīrati Khayril 'Ibād* in which he compiled from over three hundred sources.

"Jibrīl."

"Who is with you?

"Muḥammad."

"Has he been sent for?"

"Yes."

"Welcome to him, from his family! May Allāh grant him long life, a brother and deputy, and what excellent brother and deputy! What an excellent visit this is!"

The gate was opened. When they came in, they saw Prophet Idrīs ﷺ. Allāh ﷻ exalted him to a lofty place. The Prophet ﷺ greeted him and he returned his greeting and said:

> "Welcome to the righteous brother and the righteous Prophet!" Then he invoked for goodness on his behalf.

The Fifth Heaven[38]

Then they ascended to the Fifth Heaven. Angel Jibrīl ﷺ asked for the gate to be opened. Someone said:

"Who is this?"

"Jibrīl."

"Who is with you?

"Muḥammad."

"Has he been sent for?"

"Yes."

"Welcome to him, from his family! May Allāh grant him long life,

38 Imām Najmuddīn Al-Ghayṭī: *Al-Ibtihāj fil-Kalām 'alal-Isrā' wal Mi'rāj* by the Ḥadith scholar Najmuddīn Abul Mawāhib Muḥammad ibn Aḥmad ibn 'Alī ibn Abī Bakr Al-Ghayṭī As-Sakandarī al-Miṣrī al-Shāfi'ī (d. 981). See Imām Al-Kattānī, *al-Risāla al-Mustaṭrafa.* Imām Najmuddīn Al-Ghayṭī's work was published under the title *Mawsū'at al-Isrā' wal Mi'rāj al-Mūsāmmāt Taṭrīz ad-Dībāj bi-Ḥaqā'iq al-Isrā' wal Mi'rāj* (Beirut: Dār wa Maktabat al-Hilāl, 1994).

a brother and deputy, and what excellent brother and deputy! What an excellent visit this is!"

The gate was opened. When they came in they saw Prophet Hārūn ﷺ. Half of his beard was white and the other half was black. It almost reached his navel due to its length. Surrounding him were a company of the children of Bani Isrā'īl listening to him as he was telling them a story. The Holy Prophet ﷺ greeted him and he returned his greeting and said: "Welcome to the righteous brother and the righteous Prophet!" Then he invoked for goodness on his behalf.

The Prophet ﷺ asked:

"Who is this, O Jibrīl?"

He (*Jibrīl*) replied:

"This is the man beloved among his people, Hārūn Ibn 'Imrān."

The Sixth Heaven[39]

Then they ascended to the Sixth Heaven. Jibrīl ﷺ asked for the gate to be opened. Someone said:

"Who is this?"

"Jibrīl."

"Who is with you?

"Muḥammad."

"Has he been sent for?"

"Yes."

39 The Noble Scholar, His Eminence Shaykh Muḥammad Ibn 'Alawi Ibn 'Abbās Ibn 'Abdul 'Aziz Al-Mālikī Al-Ḥasanī Al-Makkī, Shaykhul Islam fil Baladil Ḥarām. The title of his book is: Al-Anwār al-Bahiyyah min Isrā' wa Mi'rāj Khayril Bariyyah, "The Resplendent Lights of the Night-Journey and Ascension of the Best of Creation," (Makkah, 1414/1993). Translated by Shaykh Gibril Fouad Haddad.

"Welcome to him, from his family! May Allāh grant him long life, a brother and deputy, and what excellent brother and deputy! What an excellent visit this is!"

The gate was opened. The Prophet ﷺ passed by Prophets who had with them less than ten followers in all, while others had a large company, and others had not even one follower.

Then he saw a huge dark mass (سَوَاد عَظِيم – *sawād 'aẓīm*) that was covering the firmament. He ﷺ said:

"What is this thing?"

Jibrīl ﷺ said:

"This is Mūsā and his people. Now raise your head and look."

He raised his head and saw another huge dark mass that was covering the firmament from every direction he looked. Jibrīl ﷺ said:

"These are your Community (Ummah), and besides these there are seventy thousand of them that will enter Paradise without giving account."

As they went in, the Prophet ﷺ saw Mūsā Ibn 'Imrān ﷺ, a tall man with brown complexion, similar to one of the Shanū'ah, the Yemeni Tribe of pure lineage and manly virtue, with abundant hair. If he had two shirts on him, still his hair would exceed them. The Prophet ﷺ greeted him and he returned his greeting and said:

"Welcome to the righteous brother and the righteous Prophet!"

Then he (*Mūsā*) invoked for goodness on his behalf and said:

"The people claim that among the sons of Ādam I am more honoured by Allāh than this one, but it is he who is more honoured by Allāh than me!"

When the Prophet ﷺ reached him, Mūsā ﷺ wept. He was asked:
"What is it that makes you weep?"

He (*Mūsā*) replied:

"I weep because a child that was sent after me will cause more people to enter Paradise from his Community than will enter from mine. The children of Bani Isra'īl claim that among the children of Ādam I am the one most honored by Allāh, but here is one man among the children of Ādam who has come after me in the world while I am in the next world, and is more honored. If he were only by himself, I would not mind, but he has his Community (Ummah) with him!"

The Seventh Heaven[40]

Then they ascended to the Seventh Heaven. Sayyidunā Jibrīl ﷺ asked for the gate to be opened. Someone said:

"Who is this?"

"Jibrīl."

"Who is with you?

"Muḥammad."

"Has he been sent for?"

"Yes."

---

40 Imām Ash-Shāmī: *Al-Ayāt al-'Aẓīmat al-Bāhira fī Mi'rāj Sayyid Ahlid Dunyā wal Ākhirah* ﷺ by the Ḥadīth Master Shamsuddīn Muḥammad ibn Yūsuf ibn 'Alī Ash-Shāmī Ad-Dimashqī As-Ṣāliḥī Ash-Shāfi'i Nazīl al-Qāhira (d. 942).
He is Imām Suyūṭī's student. He is the author of a ten-volume biography of the Prophet ﷺ titled *Subul al-Hudā wal Rashād fī Sīrati Khayril 'Ibād* in which he compiled from over three hundred sources.

"Welcome to him, from his family! May Allāh grant him long life, a brother and deputy, and what excellent brother and deputy! What an excellent visit this is!"

The gate was opened. The Prophet ﷺ saw Prophet Ibrāhīm ؑ the Friend of Allāh (خَلِيلُ اللَّهِ – Khalīlullāh) sitting at the gate of Paradise on a throne of gold the back of which was leaning against the Inhabited House (Al-Baytul Maʿmūr). With him were a company of his people. The Prophet ﷺ greeted him and he returned his greeting and said:

> "Welcome to the righteous son[41] and the righteous Prophet!"

The Seedlings of Jannah

Then Sayyidunā Ibrāhīm ؑ said:

> "Order your Community (Ummah) to increase their Seedlings of Jannah for its soil is fertile and its land is plentiful."

The Prophet ﷺ said:

> "What are the Seedlings of Jannah?"

He (*Sayyidunā Ibrahīm*) replied:

لَا حَوْلَ وَلَا قُوَّةَ إِلَّا بِٱللَّهِ ٱلْعَلِيِّ ٱلْعَظِيمِ

"*Lā Ḥawla wa lā quwwata ilā billāhil ʿAlīyil ʿAẓīm*
There is no Power and no Strength except with Allāh the Exalted, the Almighty!"

---

41 Prophet Ibrāhīm ؑ greeted the Holy Prophet ﷺ as "My Son", and not "My Brother", because Prophet Ibrāhīm ؑ is Abul Anbiyā (أَبُو ٱلْأَنْبِيَاءِ), the Spiritual Father of All the Prophets.

Another version says:

> "Convey my greetings to your Community and tell them that Paradise has excellent soil and sweet water, and that its seedlings are:
>
> سُبْحَانَ ٱللَّهِ – **Subḥānallāh**: *Glory be to Allāh!*
> وَالْحَمْدُ لِلَّهِ – **Wal ḥamdu lillāh**: *and all Praise is for Allāh!*
> وَلاَ إِلَهَ إِلاَّ اللّٰه – **Wa lā ilāha illallāh**: *and there is no God but Allāh!*
> وَاللّٰهُ أَكْبَرُ – **Wallāhu Akbar**: *and Allāh is the Greatest!*[42]

With Prophet Ibrāhīm ﷺ were sitting a company of people with pristine faces similar to the whiteness of a blank page, and next to them were people with something in their faces. The latter stood and entered a river in which they bathed. Then they came out having purified some of their hue. Then they entered another river and bathed and came out having purified some more. Then they entered a third river and bathed and purified themselves and their hue became like that of their companions. They came back and sat next to them.

The Prophet ﷺ said:

> "O Jibrīl, who are those with white faces and those who

42 We recommend you recite the combined form:
"*Subḥānallāhi Wal ḥamdu lillāhi Wa lā ilāha illallāhu Wallāhu Akbaru, wa lā Ḥawla wa lā quwwata ilā billāhil 'Alīyil 'Aẓīm*
Glory be to Allāh! and all Praise is for Allāh! and there is no God but Allāh! and Allāh is the Greatest! And there is no Power and no Strength except with Allāh the Exalted, the Almighty!"

had something in their faces, and what are these rivers in which they entered and bathed?"

He (*Jibrīl*) replied:

"The ones with white faces are a people who never tarnished their belief with injustice or disobedience; those with something in their faces are a people who would mix good deeds with bad ones, then they repented and Allāh relented towards them. As for these rivers, the first is Allāh's mercy (*Raḥmatullāh*), the second His favor (*Ni'matullāh*), the third:

وَسَقَاهُمْ رَبُّهُمْ شَرَابًا طَهُورًا ﴿٢١﴾

(wa saqāhum rabbuhum sharāban ṭahūrā)."[43]

and their Lord gave them a pure beverage to drink

(Sūrah Al-Insān, 76:21)

Then the Prophet ﷺ was told:

"This is your place and the place of your Community (Ummah)."

He saw that his Community were divided into two halves: one half were wearing clothes that seemed as white as a blank page, the other were wearing clothes that seemed the colour of ashes or dust.

43 Qur'ān, Sūratul Insān, Chapter 76, Āyah 21.

Chapter 10

Al-Baytul Maʿmūr: The Kaʿbah In The Heaven

The Oft-Visited House –The Inhabited House[44]

The Holy Prophet Rasūlallāh ﷺ said that he was shown Al-Baytul Maʿmūr which is a Kaʿbah in heaven encompassed daily by seventy thousand angels, so that the angels who once performed Ṭawāf around it will not get a second opportunity to do so.

He entered Al-Baytul Maʿmūr (the Inhabited House) and those who were wearing the white clothes entered with him. Those that wore ash-coloured clothes were no longer able to see him, and yet they were in the best of states.

44 Imām Najmuddīn Al-Ghayṭī: *Al-Ibtihāj fil-Kalām ʿalal-Isrāʾ wal Miʿrāj* by the Ḥadith scholar Najmuddīn Abul Mawāhib Muḥammad ibn Aḥmad ibn ʿAlī ibn Abī Bakr Al-Ghayṭī As-Sakandarī al-Miṣrī al-Shāfiʿī (d. 981). See Imām Al-Kattānī, *al-Risāla al-Mustaṭrafa.* Imām Najmuddīn Al-Ghayṭī's work was published under the title *Mawsūʿat al-Isrāʾ wal Miʿrāj al-Mūsāmmāt Taṭrīz ad-Dībāj bi-Ḥaqāʾiq al-Isrāʾ wal Miʿrāj* (Beirut: Dār wa Maktabat al-Hilāl, 1994).

The Prophet ﷺ prayed in Al-Baytul Maʿmūr together with those of the believers that were with him. Every day seventy thousand Angels enter the Inhabited House, who shall never return to it until the Day of Resurrection. The Angels who have entered it never see it again, because there are so many Angels waiting for their turn to perform Ṭawāf around this Kaʿbah in the Heaven. This House is exactly superposed to the Kaʿbah in the Holy City of Makkah. If one stone fell from it, it would fall on top of the Kaʿbah.

Chapter 11

Sidratul Muntahā: The Lote Tree Of The Utmost Boundary

The Sidratul Muntahā is literally Nabk tree, or Christ-thorn tree, or Lote Tree, or Lotus Tree. It is stationed at the last extremity of the Cosmos. Al-Muntahā literally means "utmost limit". The Lote-Tree is mentioned in the Holy Qur'ān in Sūrah An-Najm.

Almighty Allāh ﷻ says:

فَأَوْحَىٰٓ إِلَىٰ عَبْدِهِۦ مَآ أَوْحَىٰ ﴿١٠﴾
مَا كَذَبَ ٱلْفُؤَادُ مَا رَأَىٰٓ ﴿١١﴾
أَفَتُمَـٰرُونَهُۥ عَلَىٰ مَا يَرَىٰ ﴿١٢﴾
وَلَقَدْ رَءَاهُ نَزْلَةً أُخْرَىٰ ﴿١٣﴾
عِندَ سِدْرَةِ ٱلْمُنتَهَىٰ ﴿١٤﴾

10. And He revealed unto His servant that which He revealed.
11. The heart lied not (in seeing) what it saw.

12. Will you then dispute with him concerning what he saw?
13. And surely he saw him yet another time.
14. By the lote-tree of the utmost boundary.

The reason why it is called "the Lote-tree beyond which none may pass" is given in the Ḥadīth narrated by Masʿūd and reported by Imām Muslim:

> "Jibrīl took me as far as the Lote-tree, beyond which none may pass. Anything which comes up from earth stops there and is taken from there, and anything which comes down from the region beyond stops there."

Imām An-Nawawī said: "It is called the Lote-tree beyond which none may pass because the knowledge of the angels stops there. No-one has gone beyond it except the Prophet Muḥammad ﷺ."

Imām Al-Qurṭubī said in Al-Mufahham: "The Ḥadīth of Anas would seem to indicate that it is in the seventh heaven, because after mentioning the seventh heaven, the Prophet ﷺ said: "Then he took me up to the Lote-tree..."

According to the Ḥadīth of Abū Dharr, it was "veiled in colours indescribable." According to the report of Thābit from Anas, narrated by Muslim, "When it was veiled with whatever it was veiled with by the command of Allāh, it changed, and no creature of Allāh can describe it because it is so beautiful."

Ibn Daḥyah said: "The Lote-tree alone was chosen, because it has three attributes - extensive shade, delicious food and beautiful scent. These attributes symbolise faith, which combines speech, actions, and intentions. The shade represents action, the food represents intention, and the scent represents speech.

Some Additional Details[45] Relating To Sidratul Muntahā – The Lote-Tree Of The Utmost Boundary

The Holy Prophet Rasūlallāh ﷺ was raised up to the Lote-tree of the Farthest Limit (Sidratul Muntahā). There ends whatever ascends from the earth before it is seized, and whatever descends from above before it is seized. Anything which comes up from earth stops there, and anything which comes down from the region beyond stops there.

It is a tree from the base of which issue rivers whose water is never brackish[46], and rivers of milk whose taste does not change after it is drunk, and rivers of wine which does not intoxicate and brings only pleasure to those who drink it, and rivers of purified honey.

Someone on his mount could travel under its shade for seventy years and still not come out of its shade. The lotus fruit that grows on it resembles the jars of Ḥijar [near Madīnah]. Its leaves are shaped like the ears of the she-elephant, and each leaf could wrap up this Community (Ummah) entirely.

The leaves of the Lote Tree could wrap up all creatures. On top of each leaf there was an angel who covered it with colours which cannot be described. Whenever he covered it by Allāh's ﷻ order it

---

45 From the Noble Scholar, His Eminence Shaykh Muḥammad Ibn 'Alawi Ibn 'Abbās Ibn 'Abdul 'Aziz Al-Mālikī Al-Ḥasanī Al-Makkī, Shaykhul Islam fil Baladil Ḥarām. The title of his book is: Al-Anwār al-Bahiyyah min Isrā' wa Mi'rāj Khayril Bariyyah, "The Resplendent Lights of the Night-Journey and Ascension of the Best of Creation," (Makkah, 1414/1993). Translated by Shaykh Gibril Fouad Haddad.

46 It does not change in taste, or color or smell, and the sweat (perspiration) of those who drink it in Paradise has the fragrance of Musk.

would change. It would turn into sapphire (يَاقُوْتْ – yāqūt) and chrysolite (زَبَرْجَد – zabarjad), the beauty of which is impossible for anyone to praise according to its merit. On it alighted moths of gold.

From the base of the tree issued four [more] rivers: two hidden rivers and two visible rivers. The Prophet ﷺ asked:

> "What are these, O Jibrīl?

He (*Jibrīl*) replied:

> "As for the hidden rivers, they are two rivers of Paradise. The visible ones are the Nile and the Euphrates."[47]

Imām Ash Shāmī said: At the base of the tree ran a source called Salsabīl. From it issued two rivers: one is the Kawthar.

The Holy Prophet ﷺ said:

> "I saw it flowing impetuously, roaring, at the speed of arrows. Near it were pavilions of pearl (لُؤْلُؤْ – *lu' lu'*), sapphire (يَاقُوْتْ – *yāqūt*), and chrysolite (زَبَرْجَد – *zabarjad*) on top of which nested green birds more delicate than any you have ever seen. On its banks were vessels of gold and silver. It ran over pebbles made of sapphire and emerald (زُمُرُّد – *zumurrud*). Its water was whiter than milk."

The Prophet ﷺ took one of the vessels and scooped some water

---

47 Imām Ibn Kathīr said: "What is meant by this – and Allāh knows best – is that these two rivers (the Nile and the Euphrates) resemble the rivers of Paradise in their purity, sweetness, fluidity, and such of their qualities. As the Prophet ﷺ said in the ḥadīth narrated by Abū Hurayrah: ' al-'ujwatu minal jannah, The Ajwah Date [of Madīnah] is from Paradise.' That is: it resembles the fruit of Paradise, not that it itself originates in Paradise. Similarly, the source of origin of these two rivers (the Nile and the Euphrates) is on earth."

and drank. It was sweeter than honey and more fragrant than musk. Angel Jibrīl ﷺ said to him:

> "This is the river which Allāh has given you as a special gift. The other river is the River of Mercy."

The Prophet ﷺ bathed in it and his past and future sins were forgiven.

At the Lote-tree of the Farthest Limit (Sidratul Muntahaa) the Holy Prophet ﷺ saw Angel Jibrīl ﷺ in his full angelic form. He had six hundred wings. Every single wing could cover the entire firmament. From his wings embellishments were strewn in all directions, such as rare pearls and sapphires of a kind Allāh ﷻ alone knows. Then the Prophet ﷺ was taken to the Kawthar and saw Jannah. Lo and behold! It contains what no eye has seen, nor ear heard, nor human mind ever imagined. On its gate he saw written:

الصَّدَقَةُ بِعَشْرِ أَمْثَالِهَا
وَالْقَرْضُ بِثَمَانِيَةَ عَشَرَ

Aṣ-ṣadaqatu bi ʿashri amthāliha
Wal qarḍu bi thamāniyati ʿashara

"Charity is repaid tenfold, and loan eighteen-fold."

The Prophet ﷺ said:

> "O Jibrīl, how can the loan be more meritorious than charity?"

He (*Jibrīl*) replied:

> "Because one asking for charity may still have some need left, while the borrower does not borrow except his need is fulfilled."

The Prophet ﷺ continued to travel until he reached rivers of milk whose taste does not change, and rivers of wine which does not intoxicate and bring only pleasure to those who drink it, and rivers of honey purified. Overhanging those rivers were domes of hollowed pearls whose circumference is as wide as the Aquarius star.

Above the rivers were pommels resembling the hides of humped camels. Its birds were like the Bactrian camel. Upon hearing this, Abū Bakr ﷺ said:

> "O Messenger of Allāh, they are certainly delicate!"

The Prophet ﷺ replied:

> "And daintier to eat yet, and I hope that you shall eat from them."[48]

The Prophet ﷺ then saw the Kawthar and on its banks were domes of hollowed pearls. The soil of its banks was extremely fragrant musk.

Then the Fire was shown to him. In it he saw Allāh's ﷻ wrath and His punishment and sanction. If rocks and iron were to be thrown into it, the Fire would consume them completely.

In it were a people who were eating carrion. The Prophet ﷺ said:

> "Who are these, O Jibrīl?"

He (*Jibrīl*) replied:

> "Those who ate the flesh of people."

---

48 This is an indication of the rank of Sayyidunā Abū Bakr ؓ in Paradise, as the Prophet's ﷺ hope, like his petition, is accepted by Almighty Allāh . Shaykh Muḥammad Ibn 'Alawī Al-Mālikī also said: "From all this it can be known that Paradise and the Fire exist already, and that the Lote-tree of the Farthest Boundary is outside Paradise."

Then the Prophet ﷺ saw the Angel Mālik ﷺ, the custodian of the Fire. He was a grim figure whose face expressed anger. He greeted the Holy Prophet, and the Prophet ﷺ greeted him. Then the gates of the Fire were closed as he stood outside, and he was raised up beyond the Lote-tree of the Farthest Limit, and a cloud concealed him from everything else, and Jibrīl ﷺ stayed back.

Chapter 12

Everyone Has His Appointed Position or Rank

When Prophet Muḥammad ﷺ reached the lote-tree, with Jibrīl ؑ still accompanying him, Jibrīl ؑ stopped. He said he could not proceed any further.

The Prophet ﷺ said to his companion:

> "O Jibrīl, I am your guest this night. Is it befitting for the host to abandon his guest? Is this a place where a friend will abandon his friend?"

To this passionate plea, Jibrīl ؑ advanced his explanation.

He (*Jibrīl*) quoted the Qur'ānic verse:[49]

49 The Holy Qur'ān, Surah As-Ṣaffāt, Chapter 37, Ayah 164.

وَمَا مِنَّا إِلَّا لَهُۥ مَقَامٌ مَّعْلُومٌ ﴿١٦٤﴾

Wa mā minnā illā lahu maqāmum maʿlūm

And there is not one of us (Angels), but has his known place (or position or rank)

"There is no one of us but has his appointed place (or rank) !

(Sūrah As-Ṣāffāt, 37:164)

The Archangel Jibrīl ﷺ said:

> "If I were to proceed one step (the size of an ant) further, I would burn... but if you were to proceed, O Muḥammad, you would pass through..."

The Prophet ﷺ asked:

> "O Jibrīl, do you need anything from your Lord?"

Jibrīl ﷺ replied:

> "Yes. If you reach where no one has ever reached, and it is said to you, here you are and here I am, then MENTION ME TO YOUR LORD !!"

It is reported that Jibrīl ﷺ pushed the Prophet ﷺ forward. The Prophet ﷺ felt very much his isolation and was troubled and most apprehensive. It was the first time, since the beginning of Israa' and Miʿraaj that he found himself alone, unaccompanied by Jibrīl ﷺ. His protestation to Jibrīl ﷺ was of no avail. He knew that from then on he must be on his own.

Jibrīl ﷺ pushed the Prophet ﷺ forward and he was thus pushed through seventy thousand Veils of light. The Prophet ﷺ was wrapped and carried in the mist of a mighty cloud, traversing immense, indescribable distances, at the end of which he found himself prostrating in front of the Throne of his Lord.

This Third Mode of Transportation used by the Holy Prophet ﷺ on the Miraculous Journey is called the RafRaf (رَفْرَفٍ). It was used for travel between the Sidratul Muntahā and the ʿArsh of Almighty Allāh ﷻ.

Chapter 13
The Conversation (Munājāt) with Almighty Allāh ﷻ

The RafRaf is the Third Mode of Transportation used by the Holy Prophet ﷺ on the Miraculous Journey. It was used by the Holy Prophet ﷺ for travel between the Sidratul Muntahā and the 'Arsh of Almighty Allāh ﷻ.

The Holy Prophet ﷺ travelled through Seventy Thousand Veils of light. The Prophet ﷺ was wrapped and carried in the mist of a mighty cloud, traversing immense, indescribable distances, at the end of which he found himself prostrating in front of the Throne of his Lord.

Here the Holy Prophet ﷺ was greeted by Allāh ﷻ, and the Messenger ﷺ responded with the words which are repeated by every Muslim in his daily prayer when sitting for Tashahhud after performing the second rak'ah :

Prophet Muḥammad ﷺ said:

التَّحِيَّاتُ لِلّهِ، وَالصَّلَوَاتُ وَالطَّيِّبَاتُ

AT-TAḤIYYĀTU LILLĀHI WAṢ-ṢALAWĀTU

WAṬ-ṬAYYIBĀTU.

"Greetings to Allāh, and all praises and reverence."

Almighty Allāh ﷻ replied:

السَّلاَمُ عَلَيْكَ أَيُّهَا النَّبِيُّ وَرَحْمَةُ اللهِ وَبَرَكَاتُهُ

AS-SALĀMU 'ALAYKA AYYUHAN-NABIYYU

WA RAḤMATULLĀHI WA BARAKĀTUH.

"Peace be upon you, O Prophet, and Mercy and Blessings of Allāh."

The Prophet ﷺ said:

السَّلاَمُ عَلَيْنَا وَعَلَى عِبَادِ اللهِ الصَّالِحِيْنَ ، أَشْهَدُ أَنْ لاَ إِلَهَ إِلاَّ اللهُ

AS-SALĀMU 'ALAYNĀ WA 'ALĀ

'IBĀDILLĀHIṢ-ṢĀLIḤEEN.

ASH-HADU AL-LĀ-ILĀHA ILLALLĀH

"Peace be upon us, and upon all the righteous servants. I bear witness that there is no deity to be worshipped except Allāh."

Almighty Allāh ﷻ continued:

وَأَشْهَدُ أَنَّ مُحَمَّدًا عَبْدُهُ وَرَسُولُهُ

WA ASH-HADU ANNA MUḤAMMADAN
'ABDUHU WA RASŪLUH

"And I bear witness that Muḥammad is His Servant and Messenger."

And then, all the angels present echoed :

اللَّهُمَّ صَلِّ عَلَىٰ مُحَمَّدٍ وَعَلَىٰ آلِ مُحَمَّدٍ

ALLĀHUMMA SALLI 'ALĀ MUḤAMMADIN
WA 'ALĀ ĀLI MUḤAMMADIN

"O Allāh, shower Your Blessings on Muḥammad and on the descendants of Muḥammad."

The Divine Meeting[50] - The Prophet's ﷺ Conversation with Almighty Allāh ﷻ
Some Additional Details

The Prophet ﷺ was taken up to a point where he heard the scratching of the Pens [writing the Divine Decree].

50 From the Noble Scholar, His Eminence Shaykh Muḥammad Ibn 'Alawi Ibn 'Abbās Ibn 'Abdul 'Aziz Al-Mālikī Al-Ḥasanī Al-Makkī, Shaykhul Islam fil Baladil Ḥarām. The title of his book is: *Al-Anwār al-Bahiyyah min Isrā' wa Mi'rāj Khayril Bariyyah*, "The Resplendent Lights of the Night-Journey and Ascension of the Best of Creation," (Makkah, 1414/1993). Translated by Shaykh Gibril Fouad Haddad.

He ﷺ saw a man who had disappeared into the light of the Throne. He ﷺ said:

> "Who is this? Is this an angel?"

It was said to him, no.

He ﷺ said:

> "Is it a Prophet?"

Again the answer was no.

He ﷺ said:

> "Who is it then?"

The answer was:

> "This is a man whose tongue was moist with Allāh's remembrance in the world, and his heart was attached to the mosques, and he never incurred the curse of his father and mother."

Then the Prophet ﷺ saw his Lord, the Most Glorious, the Exalted, and he fell prostrate. At that time his Lord spoke to him and said:

> "O Muḥammad!"

He ﷺ replied:

> "Twice at Your service, O Lord!"

Almighty Allāh ﷻ said:

> "Ask (سَلْ – *sal*)!"

The Prophet ﷺ said:

> "You have taken to Yourself Ibrāhīm as an intimate friend (خَلِيل – *Khalīl*), and You have given him an immense kingdom. You have spoken to Mūsā directly, and have given Dāwūd an immense kingdom and softened iron and subjected the mountains to him. You have given Sulaymān an immense kingdom, and subjected the Jinn and men to him, as well as the winds, and You have given him a kingdom the like of which no one may have after him. You have

taught ʿĪsā the Torah and the Injīl, and made him heal those born blind and the lepers, and raise up the dead with Your permission, and You have protected him and his mother from the cursed devil so that the devil had no path by which to harm them!"

Almighty Allāh ﷻ said:

"And I have taken you to Myself as My beloved and close friend (حَبِيباً وَ خَلِيلاً – *Ḥabīban wa khalīlan*)." The narrator said: It is written in the Torah: Ḥabībullāh "the Beloved of Allāh."[51]

---

51 This wording is in the narration from Abū Hurayrah by Imām Aṭ-Ṭabarī in his *Tafsīr* (15:10). Another wording states: "And I have taken you to Myself as My intimate friend (*khalīlī*). It is written in the Torah: *Muḥammadun Ḥabībur Raḥmān*, Muḥammad, the Beloved of the Merciful."

Also narrated from Abū Hurayrah by Al-Bazzār in his *Musnad* with a chain of trustworthy narrators except for a possible unnamed link as indicated by Imām Al-Haythamī in *Majmaʿ al-Zawāʾid* (1:71-72).

Imām Ibn Kathīr cites the latter in his Tafsīr (3:21).

Imām As-Suyūṭī in *al-Durr al-Manthūr* said that it is also narrated by Abū Yaʿlā, Muḥammad ibn Naṣr al-Marwazī in *Kitāb aṣ-Ṣalāt*, Ibn Abī Ḥātim, Ibn ʿAdī, Ibn Mardūyah, and Imām Al-Bayhaqī, in commentary of the verse:

{Glory to (Allāh) Who did take His servant for a Journey by night from the Sacred Mosque to the farthest Mosque, whose precincts We did bless,- in order that We might show him some of Our Signs: for He is the One Who heareth and seeth (all things).} (17:1).

Both wordings refute those who claim that it is preferable to call the Prophet ﷺ Khalīlullāh rather than Ḥabībullāh, as the latter (Ḥabībullāh) clearly applies only to him in the Ummah, whereas the former applies both to Prophet Ibrāhīm ﷺ and to him ﷺ, as stated in the ḥadīth narrated from Ibn Masʿūd by At-Tirmidhī (*ḥasan ṣaḥīḥ*): "Verily, your Companion – i.e. himself – is Allāh's intimate friend." This holds true regardless of the weak chain of the narration from Ibn ʿAbbās narrated by Imām Tirmidhī (gharīb) and Dārimī whereby the Prophet ﷺ said: "Lo! I am Allāh's Beloved, and I say this without pride." Further, some of the reports of the splitting of the noble breast of the Prophet quote the angels as saying to the Prophet ﷺ: "O Beloved, you shall never fear! (*Yā Ḥabīb lan turaʿ*).

In addition, the Prophet ﷺ is the foremost archetype and paradigm of the famous ḥadīth, "When Allāh loves someone, he says it to Jibrīl, etc." Qāḍi Īyād Ibn Mūsā Al-Yahsubī

Almighty Allāh ﷻ continued:

> "I have sent you for all people without exception, a bearer of glad tidings and a warner.
>
> I have expanded your breast for you, and relieved you of your burden, and exalted your name, as I am not mentioned except you are mentioned with Me.
>
> I have made your Community (Ummah) the best Community ever brought out for the benefit of mankind.
>
> I have made your Community a Middle Nation (أُمَّةً وَسَطًا – *Ummatan Wasaṭan*).
>
> I have made your Community in truth the first and the last of all Communities.
>
> I have made public address (خُطْبَة – Khuṭbah) impermissible for your Community unless they first witness that you are My servant and Messenger.
>
> I have placed certain people in your Community with Evangels for hearts (repositories for the Book of Allāh).
>
> I have made you the first Prophet created and the last one sent and the first one heard in My court.
> I have given you the Seven Oft-Repeated Verses which I gave to no other Prophet before you.[52]

---

mentioned many additional proofs in Kitāb Ash-Shifā.

52 Sūratul Fātiḥaḥ, the Opening Chapter of the Holy Qur'ān.

I have given you the last verses of Sūratul Baqarah which constitute a treasure from under My Throne which I gave to no other Prophet before you.

I have given you Al-Kawthar (ٱلْكَوْثَر).

I have given you eight lots: Islam, Emigration (ٱلْهِجْرَة *Al-Hijr*a), Striving in the way of Allāh, Charity (Ṣadaqah), Fasting in Ramadan, Ordering Good, and Forbidding Evil. The day I created the heavens and the earth I made obligatory upon you and upon your Community fifty prayers: therefore, establish them, you and your Community."

Imām Ash-Shāmī added:[53] Abū Hurayrah said that the Messenger of Allāh ﷺ said:

"My Lord has preferred me over everyone else (فَضَّلَنِي رَبِّي – *Faḍḍalanī Rabbī*). He has sent me as a mercy to the worlds and to all people without exception, a bearer of glad tidings and a warner.

He has thrown terror into the hearts of my enemies at a distance of a month's travel.

He has made spoils of war lawful for me while they were not lawful for anyone before me.

---

53 Imām Ash-Shāmī: *Al-Ayāt al-'Aẓīmat al-Bāhira fī Mi'rāj Sayyid Ahlid Dunyā wal Ākhirah* ﷺ by the Ḥadīth Master Shamsuddīn Muḥammad ibn Yūsuf ibn 'Alī Ash-Shāmī Ad-Dimashqī As-Ṣāliḥī Ash-Shāfi'i Nazīl al-Qāhira (d. 942).
He is Imām Suyūṭī's student. He is the author of a ten-volume biography of the Prophet ﷺ titled *Subul al-Hudā wal Rashād fī Sīrati Khayril 'Ibād* in which he compiled from over three hundred sources.

The entire earth was made a ritually pure place of prostration for me.

I was given the words that open, those that close, and those that are comprehensive in meaning.[54]

My Community was shown to me and there is none of the followers and the followed but he is known to me.

I saw that they would come to a people that wear hair-covered sandals.[55]

I saw that they would come to a people of large faces and small eyes as if they had been pierced with a needle.

Nothing of what they would face in the future was kept hidden from me.

And I have been ordered to perform fifty prayers daily.

And the Holy Prophet ﷺ has been given three particular merits: He is the Master of Messengers (سَيِّدُ الْمُرْسَلِين - *Sayyidul Mursalīn*), the Leader of the Godfearing (إِمَامُ الْمُتَّقِين - *Imāmul Muttaqīn*), and the Chief of Those with Signs of Light on Their Faces and Limbs (قَائِدُ الْغُرِّ الْمُحَجَّلِين – *Qā'id Al-Ghurr Al-Muḥajjalīn*).

One narration says:[56] The Prophet ﷺ was given the five

54 I was given the Apex of Eloquence. The Holy Prophet ﷺ is the Most Eloquent of all the Creation of Almighty Allāh.

55 i.e. Untanned Sandals.

56 Imām Najmuddīn Al-Ghayṭī: *Al-Ibtihāj fil-Kalām 'alal-Isrā' wal Mi'rāj* by the

daily prayers and the last verses of Sūratul Baqarah. For his sake, whoever of his Community does not associate anything with Allāh ﷻ is forgiven even the mortal sins.

Then the cloud that cloaked him was dispelled and Jibrīl ﷺ took him by the hand and sped away with him until he reached Prophet Ibrāhīm ﷺ, who did not say anything.

Then the Prophet ﷺ reached Prophet Mūsā ﷺ who asked:

"What did you do, O Muḥammad? What obligations did your Lord impose on you and your Community?"

The Holy Prophet ﷺ replied:

"He imposed fifty prayers every day and night on me and my Community."

Prophet Mūsā ﷺ said:

"Return to your Lord and ask Him to lighten your burden and that of your Community, for, in truth, your Community will not be able to carry it. Verily, I myself have experienced people's dispositions before you. I tested the Children of Israel and took the greatest pains to hold them to something easier than this, but they were too weak to carry it and they abandoned it. Those of your Community are even weaker in their bodies and constitutions, and in their hearts, their sight, and their hearing."

The Prophet ﷺ turned to Jibrīl ﷺ to consult him. Angel Jibrīl ﷺ indicated to him that yes, if he wished, then he could return.

Ḥadith scholar Najmuddīn Abul Mawāhib Muḥammad ibn Aḥmad ibn 'Alī ibn Abī Bakr Al-Ghayṭī As-Sakandarī al-Miṣrī al-Shāfi'ī (d. 981). See Imām Al-Kattānī, *al-Risāla al-Mustaṭrafa*. Imām Najmuddīn Al-Ghayṭī's work was published under the title *Mawsū'at al-Isrā' wal Mi'rāj al-Musāmmāt Taṭrīz ad-Dībāj bi-Ḥaqā'iq al-Isrā' wal Mi'rāj* (Beirut: Dār wa Maktabat al-Hilāl, 1994).

The Prophet ﷺ sped back to his Lord and then he fell prostrate. Then he ﷺ said:

> "My Lord, make lighter the burden of my Community for verily they are the weakest of all Communities."

Almighty Allāh ﷻ replied:

> "I have removed five prayers from their obligation."

Then the cloud was dispelled and the Prophet ﷺ returned to Mūsā ﷺ and told him:

> "He has removed five prayers from my obligation."

Prophet Mūsā ﷺ replied:

> "Go back to your Lord and ask him to make it less, for in truth your Community will not be able to carry that."

The Holy Prophet ﷺ did not cease to go back and forth between Mūsā and his Lord, while Almighty Allāh ﷻ each time reduced it by five prayers, until Allāh ﷻ said:

> "O Muḥammad!"

The Prophet ﷺ said:

> "Twice at Your service, O Lord!"

He (Allāh ﷻ, The Almighty) said:

> "Let them be five prayers every day and night, and let every prayer count as ten. That makes fifty prayers.
>
> This word of Mine shall not be changed nor shall My Book be abrogated. Let whoever is about to perform a good deed, even if he does not ultimately do it, receive the reward of doing it, while if he does it, he shall receive the reward tenfold.
>
> Let whoever is about to commit a bad deed, and he does not ultimately do it, let not anything be written against him, while if he does it, let one misdeed be written against him."

Then the cloud was dispelled and the Prophet ﷺ returned to Mūsā ﷺ and told him:

> "He has removed five prayers from my obligation."

He (*Mūsā*)replied:

> "Go back to your Lord and ask him to make it less, for, in truth, your Community will not be able to carry that."

The Prophet ﷺ said:

> "I have gone back again to my Lord until I feel too shy before Him. Rather, I accept and submit."

At this a herald called out, conveying from Almighty Allāh ﷻ:

> "I have decreed My obligation and have reduced the burden of My servants."

Prophet Mūsā ﷺ then said to the Holy Prophet ﷺ:

> "Return back down in the Name of Allāh."

Chapter 14
The Descent From Heaven To Earth

After this momentous Meeting with Almighty Allāh ﷻ, the Holy Prophet ﷺ started his Descent back to earth.[57]

The Prophet ﷺ did not pass a group of angels except they said to him:

> "You must practice cupping (عَلَيْكَ بِالْحِجَامَة - *'alayka bil Ḥijāmah*)," and in another version: "Order your Community (Ummah) to apply cupping."[58]

As the Prophet ﷺ was descending he asked Jibrīl ﷺ:

> "Why did I not see any of the people of heaven except they welcomed me and smiled at me except one: I greeted him

57 From the Noble Scholar, His Eminence Shaykh Muḥammad Ibn 'Alawi Ibn 'Abbās Ibn 'Abdul 'Aziz Al-Mālikī Al-Ḥasanī Al-Makkī, Shaykhul Islam fil Baladil Ḥarām. The title of his book is: *Al-Anwār al-Bahiyyah min Isrā' wa Mi'rāj Khayril Bariyyah*, "The Resplendent Lights of the Night-Journey and Ascension of the Best of Creation," (Makkah, 1414/1993). Translated by Shaykh Gibril Fouad Haddad.

58 Cupping is the process of drawing blood from the body by scarification (scratches or superficial incisions in the skin) and the application of a cupping glass (in which a partial vacuum is created, as by heat) for relieving internal congestion and other benefits.

and he greeted me back and welcomed me, but he did not smile at me?"

He (*Jibrīl*) replied:

"That was Mālik ﷺ the custodian of the Fire of Hell. He never smiled once since the day he was created. If he had ever smiled for anyone, it would have been you."

When the Prophet ﷺ reached the nearest heaven, he looked below and he saw a dense cloud of smoke filled with clamour. He ﷺ asked:

"What is this, O Jibrīl?"

He (*Jibrīl*) replied:

"These are the devils that swarm over the eyes of human beings so that they will not think about the dominions of the heavens and the earth, or else they would have seen wonders."[59]

Then he (the Holy Prophet ﷺ) mounted the Burāq again (which Sayyidunā Jibrīl ﷺ 'alayhis salām had tied in Jerusalem) and departed for Makkah.

He passed by a caravan of the Quraysh on its way back to Makkah, and he saw a camel upon which were tied two containers, a black one and a white one. When he came face to face with the caravan there was a stampede in which the caravan turned around and that

---

59 Imām Ash-Shāmī: *Al-Ayāt al-'Aẓīmat al-Bāhira fī Mi'rāj Sayyid Ahlid Dunyā wal Ākhirah* ﷺ by the Ḥadīth Master Shamsuddīn Muḥammad ibn Yūsuf ibn 'Alī Ash-Shāmī Ad-Dimashqī As-Ṣāliḥī Ash-Shāfi'i Nazīl al-Qāhira (d. 942).
He is Imām Suyūṭī's student. He is the author of a ten-volume biography of the Prophet ﷺ titled *Subul al-Hudā wal Rashād fī Sīrati Khayril 'Ibād* in which he compiled from over three hundred sources.

camel was thrown down to the ground and its freight broke.[60]

Then the Prophet ﷺ passed by another caravan that had lost one of its camels. The Prophet ﷺ directed them to where the stray camel was, and the tribe rounded it up.

The Prophet ﷺ greeted them and one of them said:

"This is the voice of Muḥammad!"

The Holy Prophet ﷺ continued on his journey and returned to his Companions in Makkah shortly before morning.

60 Imām Najmuddīn *Al-Ghayṭī: Al-Ibtihāj fil-Kalām 'alal-Isrā' wal Mi'rāj* by the Ḥadith scholar Najmuddīn Abul Mawāhib Muḥammad ibn Aḥmad ibn 'Alī ibn Abī Bakr Al-Ghayṭī As-Sakandarī al-Miṣrī al-Shāfi'ī (d. 981). See Imām Al-Kattānī, *al-Risāla al-Mustaṭrafa*. Imām Najmuddīn Al-Ghayṭī's work was published under the title *Mawsū'at al-Isrā' wal Mi'rāj al-Mūsāmmāt Taṭrīz ad-Dībāj bi-Ḥaqā'iq al-Isrā' wal Mi'rāj* (Beirut: Dār wa Maktabat al-Hilāl, 1994).

Chapter 15
The Morning After

The Holy Prophet Rasūlallāh ﷺ arrived back in Makkah after this Momentous, Miraculous Night.

When morning came, he remained alone and, knowing that people would call him a liar, sat despondently near to the Ka'bah.[61]

Allāh's ﷻ enemy, Abū Jahl, was passing by and he approached and sat down next to the Prophet ﷺ, saying by way of mockery:

"Has anything happened?"

The Prophet ﷺ replied:

"Yes."

Abū Jahl said:

"And what is that?"

The Prophet ﷺ replied:

"I was taken on a Night-Journey last night." Abū Jahl said:

"Where to?"

---

61 From the Noble Scholar, His Eminence Shaykh Muḥammad Ibn 'Alawi Ibn 'Abbās Ibn 'Abdul 'Aziz Al-Mālikī Al-Ḥasanī Al-Makkī, Shaykhul Islam fil Baladil Ḥarām. The title of his book is: *Al-Anwār al-Bahiyyah min Isrā' wa Mi'rāj Khayril Bariyyah*, "The Resplendent Lights of the Night-Journey and Ascension of the Best of Creation," (Makkah, 1414/1993). Translated by Shaykh Gibril Fouad Haddad.

The Prophet ﷺ replied:

"To the Hallowed House."

Abū Jahl said:

"Then you woke up here among us?"

The Prophet ﷺ replied:

"Yes."

Abū Jahl decided not to belie the Prophet ﷺ, fearing that the Prophet ﷺ would deny having said this to him if he went and told the people of Makkah, so he said:

"What do you think if I called your people here? Will you tell them what you just told me?"

The Prophet ﷺ said yes. Abū Jahl cried out:

"O tribe of the Children of Kaʿb ibn Luʾay, come hither!"

People left their gatherings and came until they all sat next around the two of them. Abū Jahl said:

"Tell your people what you just told me."[62]

The Messenger of Allāh ﷺ said:

"I was taken on a Night-Journey last night."

They said:

"To where?"

The Prophet ﷺ replied:

"To the Hallowed House."

They said:

"Then you woke up here among us?"

The Prophet ﷺ replied:

"Yes."

---

62 Imām Ash-Shāmī: *Al-Ayāt al-ʿAẓīmat al-Bāhira fī Miʿrāj Sayyid Ahlid Dunyā wal Ākhirah* ﷺ by the Ḥadīth Master Shamsuddīn Muḥammad ibn Yūsuf ibn ʿAlī Ash-Shāmī Ad-Dimashqī As-Ṣāliḥī Ash-Shāfiʿi Nazīl al-Qāhira (d. 942).
He is Imām Suyūṭī's student. He is the author of a ten-volume biography of the Prophet ﷺ titled *Subul al-Hudā wal Rashād fī Sīrati Khayril ʿIbād in* which he compiled from over three hundred sources.

There was no one left except he clapped his hands, or held his head in amazement, or clamoured and considered it an enormity.

Al-Muṭ'im Ibn 'Adī[63] said:

> "All of your affair before today was bearable, until what you said today. I bear witness that you are lying (ana ashhadu annaka kādhibun). We strike the flanks of the she-camels for one month to reach the Hallowed House, then for another month to come back, and you claim that you went there in one night! By al-Lāt, by al-'Uzzā![64] I do not believe you."

The people said:

> "Muḥammad, describe the Hallowed House for us. How is it built, what does it look like, how near is it to the mountain?"

There were some among them who had travelled there.

The Holy Prophet ﷺ began to describe it for them:

> "Its structure is like this, its appearance like this, its proximity to the mountain is such-and-such," and he did not stop describing it to them until he began to experience doubts about the description. He was seized with an anxiety he had not felt before, whereupon he was able to see the mosque in front of him. He was placed outside the gate of 'Aqīl. The people said: "How many gates does the mosque have?" He had not counted them before. He looked at the gates and began to count them one by one, informing them.[65]

---

63 He opposed the Holy Prophet ﷺ and died a disbeliever.

64 Al-Lāt and Al-'Uzzā were the two main idols at the Ka'bah that the Quraysh worshipped.

65 Imām Najmuddīn Al-Ghayṭī: Al-Ibtihāj fil-Kalām 'alal-Isrā' wal Mi'rāj by the Ḥadith scholar Najmuddīn Abul Mawāhib Muḥammad ibn Aḥmad ibn 'Alī ibn Abī Bakr

The people who had visited Masjidul Aqṣā before said:

"As for the description, then, by Allāh, he is correct."

Then they said:

"O Muḥammad, tell us about our caravans!"

The Prophet ﷺ replied:

"I saw a caravan as I was coming back. They had lost one of their camels and were searching for it everywhere. I reached their mounts and there was no one with them. I found a water bottle and I drank from it.[66]

Then I reached the caravan of the tribe of So-and-so in such- and-such a place. I saw a red camel carrying one black container and one white one. When I came face to face with the caravan there was a stampede and that camel fell and its freight broke.

Then I reached the caravan of the tribe of So-and-so in At-Tan'īm. It was headed by a grayish camel on which was a black hair-cloth and two blackish containers and here are the [three] caravans about to reach you from the mountain pass."

They said:

"When will they arrive?"

Al-Ghayṭī As-Sakandarī al-Miṣrī al-Shāfi'ī (d. 981). See Imām Al-Kattānī, al-Risāla al-Mustaṭrafa. Imām Najmuddīn Al-Ghayṭī's work was published under the title Mawsū'at al-Isrā' wal Mi'rāj al-Mūsāmmāt Taṭrīz ad-Dībāj bi-Ḥaqā'iq al-Isrā' wal Mi'rāj (Beirut: Dār wa Maktabat al-Hilāl, 1994).

66 Shaykh Muḥammad Ibn 'Alawī Al-Mālikī said: "Doubt has been raised about this report on the basis of the question how could the Prophet ﷺ allow himself to drink the water without permission from its owner? The answer is that he acted according to the custom of the Arabs whereby they never refuse milk (or water) to whomever passes by and takes it, and they used to instruct the herdsmen not to prevent wayfarers from taking milk from the herd (i.e. without asking the owner). And this applies to water as well.

The Holy Prophet ﷺ replied:

"On the fourth day of the week."

On that day the Quraysh came out, expecting the caravans. The day passed and they did not arrive. The Prophet ﷺ made an invocation and the day was extended one more hour during which the sun stood still, and the caravans came.

They went to meet the riders of the first caravan and asked them:

"Did you lose a camel?"

They said yes.

They asked the second caravan:

"Did one red camel of yours shatter her freight?"

They said yes.

They asked [the first caravan]:

"Did anyone lose a water bottle?"

One man said:

"I did, by Allāh, I had prepared it but none of us drank it nor was it spilled on the ground!"

At this they accused the Prophet ﷺ of sorcery and said:

"Al-Walīd spoke the truth!"[67]

---

67 Ibn Hishām narrates in his Sīrah that when the Makkan Fair was due, a number of the Quraysh came to Al-Walīd Ibn Al-Mughīrah, who was a man of some standing among the Quraysh, and he addressed them in those words:

"The time of the Fair has come round again, and representatives of the Arabs will come to you and they will have heard about this fellow of yours, so agree upon one opinion without dispute so that none will give the lie to the other." They replied: "You give us your opinion about him." He said: "No, you speak and I will listen." They said: "He is a kāhin (seer or giver of oracles)." He said: "By Allāh, he is not that, for he has not the unintelligent murmuring and rhymed speech of the kāhin." "Then he is possessed," they said. "No, he is not that," he said, "we have seen possessed ones, and here is no choking, spasmodic movements and whispering." "Then he is a poet," they said. "No, he is no poet, for we know poetry in all its forms and meters." "Then he is a sorcerer." "No, we have seen sorcerers and their sorcery,

Then Allāh ﷻ revealed the verse:

... وَمَا جَعَلْنَا ٱلرُّءْيَا ٱلَّتِىٓ أَرَيْنَٰكَ إِلَّا فِتْنَةً لِّلنَّاسِ
وَٱلشَّجَرَةَ ٱلْمَلْعُونَةَ فِى ٱلْقُرْءَانِ ۚ ...

We appointed not the vision which We showed you but as a test for mankind.

(Sūrah Al-Israa', 17:60)

---

and here is no blowing and no knots." "Then what are we to say, O Abū 'Abd al-Shams?" they asked. He replied: "By Allāh, his speech is sweet, his root is a palm-tree whose branches are fruitful, and everything you have said would be known to be false. The nearest thing to the truth is your saying that he is a sorcerer, who has brought a message by which he separates a man from his father, or from his brother, or from his wife, or from his family."

At this point they left him, and began to sit on the paths which men take when they come to the fair. They warned everyone who passed them about the Prophet's ﷺ doings.

Allāh revealed concerning al-Walīd Ibn Al-Mughīrah:

{Leave Me to deal with him whom I created lonely,
and then bestowed upon him ample means,
and sons abiding in his presence,
and made life smooth for him.
Yet he desires that I should give more.
Nay, for lo! He has been stubborn to Our revelations.
On him I shall impose a fearful doom.
For lo! He did consider; then he planned –
Self-destroyed is he, how he planned!
Again, self-destroyed is he, how he planned! –
Then looked he,
Then frowned he and showed displeasure.
Then turned he away in pride,
and said: This is naught else than magic from of old;
This is naught else than speech of mortal man.
Him shall I fling into the burning (Fire).}
(Sūrah Al-Muddaththir, 74:11-26)

ذَرْنِى وَمَنْ خَلَقْتُ وَحِيدًا (١١)
وَجَعَلْتُ لَهُۥ مَالًا مَّمْدُودًا (١٢)
وَبَنِينَ شُهُودًا (١٣)
وَمَهَّدتُّ لَهُۥ تَمْهِيدًا (١٤)
ثُمَّ يَطْمَعُ أَنْ أَزِيدَ (١٥)
كَلَّآ ۖ إِنَّهُۥ كَانَ لِءَايَٰتِنَا عَنِيدًا (١٦)
سَأُرْهِقُهُۥ صَعُودًا (١٧)
إِنَّهُۥ فَكَّرَ وَقَدَّرَ (١٨)
فَقُتِلَ كَيْفَ قَدَّرَ (١٩)
ثُمَّ قُتِلَ كَيْفَ قَدَّرَ (٢٠)
ثُمَّ نَظَرَ (٢١)
ثُمَّ عَبَسَ وَبَسَرَ (٢٢)
ثُمَّ أَدْبَرَ وَٱسْتَكْبَرَ (٢٣)
فَقَالَ إِنْ هَٰذَآ إِلَّا سِحْرٌ يُؤْثَرُ (٢٤)
إِنْ هَٰذَآ إِلَّا قَوْلُ ٱلْبَشَرِ (٢٥)
سَأُصْلِيهِ سَقَرَ (٢٦)

PART FIVE

AFTERMATH OF ISRAAʾ WAL MIʿRAAJ

Chapter 16
Response Of The People Of Makkah

When the Prophet ﷺ broke the extraordinary news of the Israa' and Mi'raaj, the people of Makkah were divided in their response.

The unbelievers found it a suitable opportunity to jeer at the Muslims and their religion. They became wildly mocking and derisive:

> Did he really say that he went to Jerusalem and came back in a single night, whereas it takes us a whole month (exhausting our camels to the point of death) to get there !!

When faced with these misgivings and the fresh campaign of slander that broke in its wake, the Prophet ﷺ gave many proofs of the factuality and truth of his account:

1. Prophet Muḥammad ﷺ told them of a caravan he had met on the road to Jerusalem, of a stray camel of theirs and how he had directed them as to where it was.

2. He told them of another caravan, which he visited while they were asleep, and how he drank of their water, not forgetting to put the lid on afterwards.

3. The people of Quraysh challenged the authenticity of this information. The Prophet told them the exact date and time when the caravan he had met on the road would return to Makkah, namely at sunrise, with a camel of a certain description at its head, that is, an Awraq (an elegant, quick-paced camel). On that day, the Quraysh were up very early in the morning and went to the outskirts of the city in the direction of Jerusalem.

> "Behold the sun has risen," shouted one of the Quraysh unbelievers.
>
> "And behold, the caravan has arrived, with the *Awraq* at their head," shouted another, "just exactly as Muḥammad foretold."

4. The Quraysh pestered the Prophet ﷺ with questions about Masjid Al-Aqṣā, where he had never gone before. The Prophet ﷺ replied by describing Masjid Al-Aqṣā in detail.

The Response of Sayyidunā Abū Bakr ؓ

The response of the faithful Believers to the Israaʾ and Miʿraaj was markedly different. The faithful Muslims, led by Abū Bakr ؓ, were very impressed and they rejoiced at this great news from their Prophet and leader. The tremendous events gave fresh, immeasurable confirmation of their faith. It gave good tidings of things yet to come, of glory and succour, after persecution and oppression.

The unbelievers came to Abū Bakr رضي الله عنه and inquired whether he believed in the truth of the story of his friend Muḥammad ﷺ, that he went to Jerusalem, then to the heavens and returned to Makkah, all in the same night ! This was before Abū Bakr رضي الله عنه had heard it from the Prophet or any of the Muslims. Abū Bakr رضي الله عنه asked:

> "Did he (the Prophet) really tell of these things?"

"Yes", they answered.

> "If he reported this news, then he has told the truth, because he never tells a lie."

The unbelievers continued:

> "Do you testify that Muḥammad went to Jerusalem and then returned within the short span of a night?"

He (*Abū Bakr*) replied:

> "Yes, I testify to that. And I testify to events even more wonder-provoking than that, (*the heavenly revelations come directly to the Prophet day and night*). His Ascension is not more astounding than that."

Because of this response, Abū Bakr رضي الله عنه was given the honorific title of *Aṣ-Ṣiddīq* (*the Testifier of the Truth*). For Abū Bakr Aṣ-Ṣiddīq رضي الله عنه, therefore, the acceptance of the Miʿraaj was just like the acceptance of the Prophethood of Muḥammad ﷺ.

Chapter 17
Obedience To Leadership

The response of Abū Bakr Aṣ-Ṣiddīq ﷺ is very meaningful and significant, and it beautifully epitomises the Islamic perspective of Almighty Allāh ﷻ, His Creation, Prophethood, Miracles, and the relationship between Muslims and their leader, the Noble Prophet Muḥammad ﷺ.

Obedience to leadership is of paramount importance in Islam. Almighty Allāh reveals to us in the Qur'ān:[68]

يَـٰٓأَيُّهَا ٱلَّذِينَ ءَامَنُوٓا۟ أَطِيعُوا۟ ٱللَّهَ وَأَطِيعُوا۟ ٱلرَّسُولَ وَأُو۟لِى ٱلْأَمْرِ مِنكُمْ ۖ فَإِن تَنَـٰزَعْتُمْ فِى شَىْءٍ فَرُدُّوهُ إِلَى ٱللَّهِ وَٱلرَّسُولِ إِن كُنتُمْ تُؤْمِنُونَ بِٱللَّهِ وَٱلْيَوْمِ ٱلْـَٔاخِرِ ۚ ذَٰلِكَ خَيْرٌ وَأَحْسَنُ تَأْوِيلًا ﴿٥٩﴾

"O you who believe, Obey Allāh, and Obey the Messenger, and those charged with authority among you. And if you differ in anything among yourselves, refer it to Allāh and His Messenger, if you believe in Allāh and the Last Day. That is best, and most suitable for final determination."

(Sūrah An-Nisā, 4:59)

68 The Holy Qur'ān, Surah An-Nisā, Chapter 4, Ayah 59.

The Prophet Muḥammad ﷺ tells us in his Ḥadīth :

> 'Abdullāh Ibn 'Umar ؓ reported that the Messenger of Allāh ﷺ said:
>
> > "It is obligatory upon a Muslim that he should listen (to the leader) and obey, whether he likes it or not, except when he is ordered to do a sinful thing. In such a case he cannot listen or obey".
> >
> > (*Agreed Upon*)

It is reported on the authority of Abū Hurayrah ؓ that the Messenger of Allāh ﷺ said:

> "It is obligatory upon you to listen and obey the orders of the leader in prosperity and in adversity, whether you are willing or unwilling, and even when someone is given preference over you".
>
> (*Muslim*)

Abū Hurayrah ؓ reported that the Messenger of Allāh ﷺ said:

> "Whoever obeys me, obeys Allāh; and he who disobeys me, disobeys Allāh; and whoever obeys my commander, obeys me; and he who disobeys my commander, disobeys me."
>
> (*Agreed Upon*)

PART SIX

COMMENTARY ON SOME ASPECTS OF THE MIʿRAAJUN NABI

Chapter 18

The Prophet's ﷺ Vision Of Allāh

Almighty Allāh reveals in Surah An-Najm, Chapter 53, Verses 1-18 :

﴿بِسْمِ اللَّهِ الرَّحْمَٰنِ الرَّحِيمِ﴾

وَٱلنَّجْمِ إِذَا هَوَىٰ ١

مَا ضَلَّ صَاحِبُكُمْ وَمَا غَوَىٰ ٢

وَمَا يَنطِقُ عَنِ ٱلْهَوَىٰٓ ٣

إِنْ هُوَ إِلَّا وَحْيٌ يُوحَىٰ ٤

عَلَّمَهُۥ شَدِيدُ ٱلْقُوَىٰ ٥

ذُو مِرَّةٍ فَٱسْتَوَىٰ ٦

وَهُوَ بِٱلْأُفُقِ ٱلْأَعْلَىٰ ٧

ثُمَّ دَنَا فَتَدَلَّىٰ ٨

فَكَانَ قَابَ قَوْسَيْنِ أَوْ أَدْنَىٰ ٩

فَأَوْحَىٰٓ إِلَىٰ عَبْدِهِۦ مَآ أَوْحَىٰ ١٠

مَا كَذَبَ ٱلْفُؤَادُ مَا رَأَىٰٓ ﴿١١﴾
أَفَتُمَـٰرُونَهُۥ عَلَىٰ مَا يَرَىٰ ﴿١٢﴾
وَلَقَدْ رَءَاهُ نَزْلَةً أُخْرَىٰ ﴿١٣﴾
عِندَ سِدْرَةِ ٱلْمُنتَهَىٰ ﴿١٤﴾
عِندَهَا جَنَّةُ ٱلْمَأْوَىٰٓ ﴿١٥﴾
إِذْ يَغْشَى ٱلسِّدْرَةَ مَا يَغْشَىٰ ﴿١٦﴾
مَا زَاغَ ٱلْبَصَرُ وَمَا طَغَىٰ ﴿١٧﴾
لَقَدْ رَأَىٰ مِنْ ءَايَـٰتِ رَبِّهِ ٱلْكُبْرَىٰٓ ﴿١٨﴾

1. By the Star when it falls,
2. Your companion errs not, nor is he deceived,
3. Nor does he speak out of (his own) desires,
4. It is naught save a WAḤY (Revelation) that is inspired,
5. Which one of mighty powers has taught him,
6. One vigorous, that was firmly established,
7. And he was on the uppermost horizon,
8. Then he drew nearer and came down,
9. Till he was (at the distance of),
Two bows length or even nearer,
10. And He revealed unto His servant that which He revealed.
11. The heart lied not (in seeing) what it saw,
12. Will you then dispute with him concerning what he saw?
13. And surely he saw him yet another time!
14. By the Lote-tree of the utmost boundary!
15. Near unto which is the Garden of Abode.
16. When that which shrouds the Lote-tree did shroud it,
17. The eye turned not aside nor yet was overbold,
18. Surely, he saw some of the greater signs of his Lord!"

This English rendering of Sūrah An-Najm (The Star), presupposes the Prophet Muḥammad ﷺ actually saw his Lord on his Miʿraaj (ascent to heaven).

This view has adherents among old as well as recent authorities. Leading among the recent authorities is Shaykh Muḥammad Mutawalli Ash-Shaʿrāwi (Raḥimahullah - May Allāh have Mercy on him). In his work on Israaʾ and Miʿraaj, Shaykh Ash-Shaʿrāwi advances the following reasons to support his view:[69]

1. Sūrah An-Najm refers to the source of Waḥy (وَحْيٌ – *Revelation*). The source of Revelation is Almighty Allāh, subḥānahu wa taʿāla. Jibrīl ʿalayhis salām is not the source of revelation, but the mere conveyor of it.

2. The verses in Sūrah An-Najm refers to the Prophet as ʿABDIHI (عَبْدِهِ – *His Slave*) indicating that the Prophet stands (vis-a-vis the source of Waḥy) in the relation of slave to master. Thus the source of the Waḥy in question cannot be Jibrīl, because the Prophet ﷺ could never be said to be a slave of Jibrīl. He is the slave of Allāh alone.

3. The verses in Sūrah An-Najm mention the fact that the polytheists among the Quraysh did not believe the Prophet's ﷺ report of Israaʾ and Miʿraaj. The vision of Jibrīl or lack of it was never the theme of that disputation. Rather it was the visiting of Jerusalem during the Israaʾ and the bodily ascension or Miʿraaj into heaven and the seeing of Allāh ﷻ. The Archangel Jibrīl ﷺ was not the issue of

69 Shaykh Muḥammad Mutawalli Ash-Shaʿrāwi (Rahimahullah - May Allāh have Mercy on him). In his book on Al-Israaʾ Wal Miʿraaj.

disagreement.

4. The Qur'ānic assurance - that the heart of the Prophet Muḥammad ﷺ did not deceive him, nor his vision turn aside, nor yet was it overbold (transgressing its limits) strongly suggests that the seeing in question was that of Almighty Allāh [subḥānahu wa ta'āla].

5. Finally, how could the seeing be that of Jibrīl, whereas the Prophet ﷺ had actually seen him, since the time of the first Qur'ānic Revelation at the cave of Ḥirā' on Jabal Nūr, and subsequently a number of times. Also he was his companion all the way from Makkah to Jerusalem and during his ascent to the heavens, during this Israa' and Mi'raaj. He had even seen him in his true shape, before the event of Israa' and Mi'raaj.

Chapter 19
The Believers And The Vision Of Allāh In This World And The Hereafter

Almighty Allāh reveals in the Holy Qur'ān:

وُجُوهٌ يَوْمَئِذٍ نَّاضِرَةٌ ﴿٢٢﴾

إِلَىٰ رَبِّهَا نَاظِرَةٌ ﴿٢٣﴾

Some faces, that Day, will beam (in brightness and beauty),[70]
Looking at their Lord (Allāh).

(Sūrah Al-Qiyāmah, 75:22-23)

كَلَّآ إِنَّهُمْ عَن رَّبِّهِمْ يَوْمَئِذٍ لَّمَحْجُوبُونَ ﴿١٥﴾

Nay! Surely they (evil-doers) will be veiled from seeing their Lord that Day.[71]

(Sūrah Al-Muṭaffifīn, 83:15)

---

70 The Holy Qur'ān, Sūratul Qiyāmah, Chapter 75, Āyah 22-23

71 The Holy Qur'ān, Sūratul Muṭaffifīn, Chapter 83, Āyah 15

Imām Mālik ﷺ referred to the above Verses, and said that this is proof of the believers' Vision of Almighty Allāh in the Hereafter (Ākhirah).[72] Some Believers will see Almighty Allāh in the Hereafter.

Imām Ibn Khafīf stated in his Al-'Aqīdah Aṣ-Saḥīḥah:[73]

> 30. The believers shall see Allāh on the Day of Resurrection just as they see the full moon on the nights when it rises. They will not be unfairly deprived of seeing Him.
>
> 31. They will see Him without encompassment (iḥāṭa) nor delimitation (taḥdīd) within any given limit (ḥadd), whether from the front, the back, above, below, right, or left.

In other words, the Believers will see Almighty Allāh in the Hereafter, without specifying "How".

The Ahlus Sunnah referred to the verses:

وُجُوهٌ يَوْمَئِذٍ نَّاضِرَةٌ ﴿٢٢﴾

إِلَىٰ رَبِّهَا نَاظِرَةٌ ﴿٢٣﴾

Some faces, that Day, will beam (in brightness and beauty),
Looking at their Lord (Allāh).

(Sūrah Al-Qiyāmah, 75:22-23)

72 Imām Ibn 'Abdul Barr mentioned this in Al-Intiqā'.

73 Shaykh Gibril Fouad Haddad, The Vision of Allāh in the World and the Hereafter.

and the mass-narrated ḥadīths on this subject, and declared that that the Believers will see Almighty Allāh in the Hereafter, the Vision will be real.

Imām Mulla 'Alī Al-Qāri and Imām Al-Haytamī reported that the agreement of Ahlus Sunnah is that sight of Almighty Allāh in the world is possible but that it does not take place, except for the Holy Prophet Rasūlallāh ﷺ.

The proof that the Sight of Almighty Allāh is possible in the world was adduced from Prophet Mūsā's ﷺ request to Allāh:

... رَبِّ أَرِنِي أَنظُرْ إِلَيْكَ ...

My Lord! Show me Your Self, that I may look (gaze) upon You[74]

(Sūrah Al-A'raf, 7:143)

And the Prophets do not ask for the impossible. Thus, it is possible for the Believers to see Almighty Allāh ﷻ.[75]

Imām Al-Qushayrī stated in the Risālah that the sight of Allāh ﷻ in the world does not take place for anyone except the Prophet – Allāh bless and greet him[76]. Al-Dhahabī also said that the sight of Allāh in the world is possible.

Among the best statements on the issue is that of Shaykh Muḥyiddīn Ibn 'Arabī: "He can be seen with the hearts and the

---

74 Qur'ān, Sūratul A'rāf, Chapter 7, Āyah 143.

75 This is stated by Imām Al-Haramayn Al-Juwaynī in Al-Irshād, p. 169.

76 Imām Al-Qushayrī, Laṭā'if Al-Ishārāt, (5:152).

eyes, if He so wills."[77]

The Prophet ﷺ saw Almighty Allāh before death as is the doctrine of the majority of Ahlus Sunnah. This is related from Imām An-Nawawī by Mulla 'Alī Al-Qāri. The evidence for this is the ḥadīth of Sayyidunā Abdullah Ibn 'Abbās whereby the Prophet ﷺ said:

"I saw my Lord" (رَأَيْتُ رَبِّي – ra'aytu rabbi).

Imām Ibn Kathīr cited this ḥadīth in his commentary on Sūrah An-Najm and declared its chain sound.

Imām Al-Bayhaqī also narrated the ḥadīth "I saw my Lord" in Al-Asma' waṣ Ṣifāt with a sound chain.

Imām Mulla 'Alī Al-Qāri commented on a similar ḥadīth whereby the Prophet ﷺ said:

> "My Lord came to me in the best form - the narrator said: I think he said: 'in my sleep' - and asked me over what did the Higher Assembly (الْمَلَأُ الأَعْلَى –Al-Mala'ul A'lā) vie for, and I said I did not know. So He put His hand between my shoulders, and I felt its coolness in my innermost being, and knowledge of all things between the East and the West came to me."

On the whole, the scholars' interpretations of the Prophet's ﷺ Vision show that whether it took place in his dream or in a wakeful state, "with the eyes of the heart" or "with the eyes of the head," does not change the fact that he saw Him in the real sense, as the Prophet's ﷺ dream-vision or heart-vision is by far sharper, more

77 This is stated in Al-Futūhāt Al-Makkiyyah, Shaykh Muhyiddīn Ibn 'Arabī. V1:162, V1:142.

accurate, and more real than the visions of ordinary people.[78]

Ahlus Sunnah scholars gave many interpretations of the above ḥadīth.

For example, al-Razi and, before him, al-Bayhaqī, interpreted the placing of Allāh's Hand as His extreme consideration and attention to the Prophet ﷺ.

Or as His immense favour to him.

While its specific placing between his shoulders refers to the pouring of divine kindness and mercy into his heart, and the coolness refers to the completion and perfection of his knowledge as shown by his words "I knew all things between the East and the West."

Imām Mulla ʿAlī Al-Qāri wrote the following in the chapter on the Prophet's ﷺ turban in his book Jamʿ al-Wasā'il fi Sharh al-Shamā'il, a commentary on al-Tirmidhi's Shama'il or "Characteristics of the Prophet":

> And Allāh knows best about the states of His Prophets and Intimate Friends whom He has raised with His most excellent upbringing, and the mirrors of whose hearts He has polished with His most excellent polish, until they witnessed the Station of Divine Presence and Abiding (المَقَام الحُضُور والبَقَاء – maqām al-ḥuḍūr wal baqā'), and they rid themselves of the rust of screens and extinction (صَدَأ الهُزُور والفَنَاء – ṣada'

78 Shaykh Gibril Fouad Haddad, The Vision of Allāh in the World and the Hereafter.

al-huzūr wal fanā').[79]

Mulla 'Alī Al-Qāri mentioned that when the Holy Prophet saw that his Lord put His hand between his shoulders, the Prophet honoured that place with the extremity of the turban.

And he added that Ibn Sadaqa said that Abū Zur'a said: "The ḥadīth of Ibn 'Abbas [about the Prophet seeing His Lord] is sound (*Ṣaḥīḥ*).

Among the Companions, Sayyidunā 'Abdullāh Ibn 'Abbas related that the Messenger of Allāh saw his Lord.

A narration by At-Tirmidhī from Ash-Sha'bī states the following:

> 'Abdullāh Ibn 'Abbas met Ka'b Al-Aḥbār in 'Arafāt and asked him about something, whereupon Ka'b began to shout "Allāhu Akbar!" until the mountains answered him.
>
> Ibn 'Abbas said:
>
> > "We are the Banū Hāshim!"
>
> Ka'b said:
>
> > "Allāh Subḥānahu wa Ta'alā has apportioned His vision and His speech between Muḥammad and Musa. Prophet Musa spoke with Allāh twice, and Prophet Muḥammad saw Allāh twice."[80]

It is authentically narrated from 'Abdullāh Ibn 'Abbas that the Prophet saw his Lord, and also authentically related that Ibn 'Abbas said: "He saw Him with his heart."

---

79 Shaykh Gibril Fouad Haddad, The Vision of Allāh in the World and the Hereafter.

80 Shaykh Gibril Fouad Haddad, The Vision of Allāh in the World and the Hereafter.

ʿAbbās's ﵁ statement that "He saw Him" does not contradict that claim, nor his statement that "He saw Him with his heart." For it is also authentically related that the Prophet ﷺ said: "I saw my Lord - glorified and exalted is He!"

Imām Aḥmad ﵀ said once: "He saw Him", and another time he said: "He saw Him with his heart." These are the two statements narrated from Imām Ahmad on the issue.

Imām Ibn Ḥajar ﵀ analysed this issue at length in his works[81] and compiled a monograph on the topic titled Al-Ghunyā fir Ru'yā.

Imām Mulla ʿAlī Al-Qāri ﵀ also gave an authoritative discussion of the topic in Al-Mirqāt.

اللَّهُمَّ صَلِّ عَلَى سَيِّدِنَا مُحَمَّدٍ وَعَلَى آلِ سَيِّدِنَا مُحَمَّدٍ

ALLĀHUMMA ṢALLI ʿALĀ SAYYIDINĀ MUḤAMMADIN WA ʿALĀ ʾĀLI SAYYIDINĀ MUḤAMMADIN

"O Allāh, shower Your Blessings on our Master Muḥammad, and on the Noble Family of our Master Muḥammad."

81 Imām Ibn Ḥajar Al-Asqalānī, Fatḥul Bārī, Sharḥ Ṣaḥīḥ Al-Bukhārī, and Al-Iṣābah.

Chapter 20

Ḥijāmah And The Mi'raajun Nabi

Ḥijāmah is mentioned emphatically in the Mi'raajun Nabi.

During the Mi'raajun Nabi, on his Descent from the Heavens to earth, the Prophet ﷺ did not pass a group of angels except they said to him:

> "You must practice Ḥijāmah (Cupping), ['Alayka bil Ḥijāmah]," and in another version: "Order your Community (Ummah) to apply Cupping."[82]

حَدَّثَنَا نَصْرُ بْنُ عَلِيٍّ الْجَهْضَمِيُّ، حَدَّثَنَا زِيَادُ بْنُ الرَّبِيعِ، حَدَّثَنَا عَبَّادُ بْنُ مَنْصُورٍ، عَنْ عِكْرِمَةَ، عَنِ ابْنِ عَبَّاسٍ، أَنَّ رَسُولَ اللَّهِ - صلى الله عليه وسلم - قَالَ " مَا مَرَرْتُ لَيْلَةَ أُسْرِيَ بِي بِمَلإٍ مِنَ الْمَلاَئِكَةِ إِلاَّ كُلُّهُمْ يَقُولُ لِي عَلَيْكَ يَا مُحَمَّدُ بِالْحِجَامَةِ " .

82 Cupping is the process of drawing blood from the body by scarification (scratches or superficial incisions in the skin) and the application of a cupping glass (in which a partial vacuum is created, as by heat) for relieving internal congestion and other benefits.

It was narrated from Ibn 'Abbas that the Messenger of Allāh ﷺ said:

> "On the night on which I was taken on the Night Journey (Isrā'), I did not pass by any group of angels but all of them said to me: 'O Muḥammad, you should use cupping.'"[83]
>
> **(Sunan Ibn Mājah, Ḥadīth: 3477)**

In the narration reported by 'Abdullāh Ibn Mas'ūd ﷺ (may Allāh be pleased with him) the angels said:

> "Oh Muḥammad, order your Ummah (nation) with Ḥijāmah."[84]
>
> **(Reported by Imām At-Tirmidhī)**

According to a ḥadīth narrated by Sayyidunā Anas Ibn Mālik ﷺ, may Allāh be pleased with him, the Prophet (peace and blessings of Allāh be upon him) said:

> "I did not pass by any group of Angels on the night when I was taken on the Journey of Isrā', but they said to me, 'O Muḥammad, tell your Ummah to do Cupping.'"[85]
>
> **(Reported by Ibn Mājah; it has corroborating evidence which strengthens it)**

The Prophet ﷺ said:

> "Jibrīl ﷺ repeatedly emphasized upon me to resort to Ḥijāmah (Cupping) to the extent that I thought that Cupping will be made compulsory."

---

83 Sunnan Ibn Mājah, Kitāb Aṭ-Ṭibb, The Book of Medicine, Chapter of Cupping, Ḥadīth #3477.

84 Sunnan Ibn Mājah, Kitāb Aṭ-Ṭibb, The Book of Medicine, Chapter of Cupping, Ḥadīth #3477.

85 This Ḥadīth is Reported by Ibn Mājah in his Sunan; it has corroborating evidence which strengthens it.

There are many wonderful benefits of Ḥijāmah.

Cupping is Among the Best of Remedies

Ḥijāmah was declared to be among the best of medicines by the Holy Prophet Muḥammad (peace and blessings be upon him).

> "If there is something excellent to be used as a remedy, then it is Ḥijāmah Cupping".[86]
> **(Narrated by Abu Hurayrah, Sunan Ibn Mājah)**

The Prophet ﷺ explained that Ḥijāmah is one of the best medicines:

> "The best medicine with which you treat yourselves is Ḥijāmah, or it is one of the best of your medicines," or "The best treatment you can use is Ḥijāmah."[87]
> **(Ṣaḥīḥ Al-Bukhārī, Ḥadīth: 5371)**

The Holy Prophet ﷺ (peace and blessings be upon him) said:

> "Cupping is the most helpful procedure for human beings to cure themselves."
> **(Ṣaḥīḥ Al-Bukhārī, Ḥadīth: 5357)**

> "The best treatment is cupping, it removes blood, lightens the back and sharpen the eyesight".
> **(Al–Hakim 4/212, At-Tirmidhī, Ḥadīth: 3053)**

In Ḥijāmah Cupping there is a Cure

The Prophet ﷺ also said:

---

86 This Ḥadīth is narrated by Sayyidunā Abu Hurayrah ؓ, and reported in Sunan Ibn Mājah.

87 This Ḥadīth is reported by Imam Bukhārī in Ṣaḥīḥ Al-Bukhārī, Ḥadīth No: 5371.

> "If there is anything good in the medicines with which you treat yourselves, it is in the incision of the Ḥijāmah therapist, or a drink of honey or cauterization with fire, but I do not like to be cauterized."[88]
> **(Ṣaḥīḥ Muslim, Ḥadīth: 2205)**

Jābir Ibn 'Abdullāh ﷺ narrated that the Messenger of Allāh ﷺ said:

> "Indeed in cupping (Ḥijāmah) there is a cure."[89]
> **(Ṣaḥīḥ Muslim, Ḥadīth: 5706)**

Best Days for Ḥijāmah

Sayyidunā Abū Hurayrah ﷺ narrated that the Messenger of Allāh ﷺ said:

> "Whoever performs Cupping (Ḥijāmah) on the 17th, 19th or 21st day (of the Islamic, lunar month) then it is a cure for every disease."[90]
> **(Sunan Abū Dawud, Ḥadīth: 3861)**

Ḥijāmah - Cupping done on the Prophet ﷺ

Sayyidunā Anas Ibn Maalik (may Allāh be pleased with him) narrated that the Messenger of Allāh ﷺ was treated with cupping (Ḥijāmah) three times, on the two veins at the side of the neck and the base of the neck.[91]

(Ṣaḥīḥ, Sunan Abu Dawud (3860), Sunan Ibn Maajah Ḥadīth: 3483)

---

88 Imām Muslim reports this Ḥadīth in Ṣaḥīḥ Muslim, Ḥadīth No: 2205.

89 Imām Muslim reports this Ḥadīth in Ṣaḥīḥ Muslim, Ḥadīth No: 5706.

90 Imām Abu Dāwūd reports this Ḥadīth in his Sunan, Ḥadīth No: 3861].

91 Imām Abu Dāwūd reports this Ḥadīth in his Sunan, Ḥadīth No: 3861. Also, Sunan Ibn Mājah, Ḥadīth No: 3483.

Ḥijāmah for Bruising

Jābir Ibn 'Abdullāh narrated that the Messenger of Allāh ﷺ fell from his horse onto the trunk of a palm tree and dislocated his foot. The Messenger of Allāh ﷺ was cupped on (his foot) for bruising."[92]

(Ṣaḥīḥ, Sunan Ibn Mājah, Ḥadīth: 2807)

Sayyidunā Anas Ibn Mālik ﷺ narrated that the Prophet ﷺ used to have Ḥijāmah done on the veins on the side of the neck and the upper back.[93]

(Reported by At-Tirmidhī)

Ḥijāmah for Headache

Sayyidunā Abdullah Ibn Abbas ﷺ narrated that the Messenger of Allāh ﷺ was cupped on his head for a serious headache while he was in Ihrām.[94]

(Ṣaḥīḥ Al-Bukhārī, Ḥadīth: 5701)

Sayyidunā Salma ﷺ the servant of the Messenger of Allāh ﷺ said:

> "Whenever someone would complain of a headache to the Messenger of Allāh ﷺ, he would advise them to perform Cupping."
>
> **(Ṣaḥīḥ; Sunan Abu Dawud, Ḥadīth: 3858)**

Ḥijāmah for Hip Pain

Sayyidunā Jābir Ibn 'Abdullāh narrated that the Messenger of Allāh ﷺ was treated with Cupping (Ḥijāmah) on his hip for a pain

92 This Ḥadīth is Reported by Ibn Mājah in his Sunan, Ḥadīth #2807, Graded Ṣaḥīḥ.

93 This Ḥadīth is reported by Imām At-Tirmidhī in his Sunan.

94 This Ḥadīth is reported by Imām At-Tirmidhī in his Sunan.

in that area.[95]
(Ṣaḥīḥ; Sunan Abu Dāwūd, Ḥadīth: 3863)

Ḥijāmah at the Top of the Head - Umm Mughīth
Sayyidunā 'Abdullāh Ibn 'Umar ﷺ narrated that the Messenger of Allāh ﷺ used to perform Ḥijāmah on his head and would call it (the place at the top of the head) "Umm Mughīth."

Ḥijāmah Done to Remove the Effect of Magic
The Messenger of Allāh ﷺ was cupped on his head when he was afflicted with magic. This is from the best of cures for this affliction, if performed correctly.
(Zādul Ma'ād (4/125-126)

Ḥijāmah For Intelligence and Memory
Sayyidunā 'Abdullāh Ibn Umar ﷺ narrated that the Messenger of Allāh ﷺ said:

> "Cupping (Ḥijāmah) on an empty stomach is best. In it is a cure and a blessing. It improves the intellect and the memory..."[96]
> **(Sunan Ibn Mājah, Ḥadīth: 3487)**

Also, Sayyidunā Abdullāh Ibn Umar ﷺ narrated that the Messenger of Allāh ﷺ said:

> "Ḥijāmah (Cupping) on an empty stomach is best.
> It increases the intellect and improves the memory.

95 This Ḥadīth is graded Ṣaḥīḥ; Reported in Sunan Abu Dāwūd, Ḥadīth #3863.
96 This Ḥadīth is Reported by Imām Ibn Mājah in his Sunan, Ḥadīth #3487.

It improves the memory of the one memorizing...."[97]
(Ṣaḥīḥ; Sunan Ibn Mājah, Ḥadīth: 3488)

Payment for Ḥijāmah (Cupping)
Sayyidunā 'Abdullāh Ibn 'Abbās ﷺ narrated that the Prophet ﷺ was treated with Cupping, and he paid the Cupper (Al-Ḥajjām) his fee."[98]
(Reported by Imām Al-Bukhārī, 10/124; Imām Muslim, 1202)

Sayyidunā Anas Ibn Mālik ﷺ narrated that the Messenger of Allāh ﷺ was treated with Cupping by Abu Ṭayyibah.

He ordered that the Cupper (Al-Ḥajjām) should be given (a payment of) two measures of food, and he spoke with the tax collectors, who reduced his taxes. The Prophet ﷺ said:

"The best treatment you can use is Cupping."[99]
(Reported by Imām Al-Bukhārī, 10/126; Imām Muslim, 1577)

97 This Ḥadīth is Reported by Imām Ibn Mājah in his Sunan, Ḥadīth #3488. Graded Ṣaḥīḥ.

98 This Ḥadīth is reported by Imām Bukhārī in Ṣaḥīḥ Al-Bukhārī, 10/124. And Imam Muslim in his Ṣaḥīḥ, 1202.

99 This Ḥadīth is reported by Imām Bukhārī in Ṣaḥīḥ Al-Bukhārī, 10/126. And Imām Muslim in his Ṣaḥīḥ, 1577.

Chapter 21

Terrible Things Seen By The Prophet ﷺ

Then the Prophet ﷺ was shown some terrible sights:

1. Those who unlawfully acquire and spend the wealth of orphans were seen swallowing balls of fire, which entered at the mouth and came out from the posterior to be swallowed again and again.

2. Those who deal in Usury (Ribā) were seen with bellies the size of big rooms filled with blazing fires.

3. Those who engage in backbiting and slander, defaming others by spreading false and vicious rumours about them, were seen eating rotten human flesh.

4. Married fornicators (*those who commit adultery*) were seen eating rotten meat, and being unable to eat cooked fresh meat.

5. Married women who entered strangers in the lineage of their husbands, by bearing and giving birth to the children of other men, were seen tortured by being hung by their breasts.

Chapter 22

Wonderful Things Seen By The Prophet ﷺ

The wonderful and consoling sights the Prophet was shown on MIʿRAAJ far outnumbered the terrible ones. These included:

1. The Burāq.

2. Masjid Al-Aqṣā.

3. The Miʿraaj.

4. He saw Angel Jibrīl (AS) in his true form, with six hundred beautiful wings of vast dimensions, covering the whole horizon and adorned with shining, precious rubies, emeralds and pearls.

5. He saw the Angel Ismāʿīl (AS), the Grand Keeper of the Doors of Heaven, with a radiant face and smiling eyes.

6. He saw the indescribable wonders of Paradise, and some

of the abodes allocated for him and his companions.

7. He saw and met the Prophets Ādam, Jesus, John, Joseph, Idrīs, Aaron, Moses, and Abraham ﷺ.

8. He was shown Al-Bayt Al-Maʿmūr (the Oft-visited House) in Jannah, and many other wonderful sights.

Chapter 23
Between Prophets Ibrāhīm ﵇ And Muḥammad ﷺ

The Prophet Ibrāhīm ﵇ is the paternal ancestor of the Prophet Muḥammad ﷺ, and for that matter, all Quraysh, the tribe of the Prophet. Thus, Ibrāhīm ﵇ parented two great nations, the Quraysh Arabs and the Israelites (who were the sons of Yaʿqūb, son of Isḥāq, son of Ibrāhīm). The lineage of the Prophet Muḥammad ﷺ, goes back to Ibrāhīm ﵇ via Ismāʿīl Ẓabīḥullāh (*the one spared from slaughter by Allāh*).

Spiritual Ancestor Of Muslims

The Muslims in general (Arabs and non-Arabs) are spiritually related to Prophet Ibrāhīm ﵇. The Holy Qur'ān describes him as the spiritual ancestor of all Muslims. Almighty Allāh says in the Holy Qur'ān:[100]

100 The Holy Qur'ān, Surah Al-Ḥajj, Chapter 22, Ayah 78.

وَجَٰهِدُواْ فِى ٱللَّهِ حَقَّ جِهَادِهِۦۚ هُوَ ٱجْتَبَىٰكُمْ وَمَا جَعَلَ عَلَيْكُمْ فِى
ٱلدِّينِ مِنْ حَرَجٍۚ مِّلَّةَ أَبِيكُمْ إِبْرَٰهِيمَۚ هُوَ سَمَّىٰكُمُ ٱلْمُسْلِمِينَ مِن قَبْلُ
وَفِى هَٰذَا لِيَكُونَ ٱلرَّسُولُ شَهِيدًا عَلَيْكُمْ وَتَكُونُواْ شُهَدَآءَ عَلَى ٱلنَّاسِۚ
[...]

"And strive in the Cause of Allāh as you ought to strive (with endeavour, sincerity and discipline). He who has chosen you, and has not imposed any difficulties on you in religion; It is the religion of your father Abraham. It is He who has named you Muslims, both before and in this (Revelation); That the Messenger may be a witness for you, and you be witnesses for mankind....."

(Sūrah Al-Hajj, 22:78)

Status Of Prophet Ibrāhīm ﵇

The Holy Prophet Muḥammad ﷺ reported his meeting with Prophet Ibrāhīm ﵇ on the seventh and last heaven. Thus, Ibrāhīm's status surpasses that of all Prophets, including Ādam and Moses ﵉, who occupied the first and sixth heaven respectively.

Physical Similarity

The Prophet ﷺ said he was struck by the physical similarity that existed between him and the father of all Prophets, Ibrāhīm ﵇.

Khalīlullāh – The Special Friend Of Allāh

As the closest friend of Allāh (Khalīlullāh), it is quite logical that Ibrāhīm ﷺ should occupy the heaven closest to the Throne of Allāh.

Chapter 24

Between Prophets Mūsā ﷺ And Muḥammad ﷺ

"The Ordinance Of Ṣalāh"

Accounts of the Israa' and Mi'raaj show us the special relationship between the Prophets Muḥammad ﷺ and Mūsā (Moses) ﷺ:

1. For one thing, the Holy Prophet Muḥammad ﷺ described the physical appearance and complexion of Moses ﷺ as one most comparable to that of the men of the Arabian tribe of Shanū'ah. In another place the Prophet ﷺ compared the physical appearance of Moses ﷺ to that of the men of the Azd tribe of Oman.

The Azd were originally Arabs from Yemen, who migrated northward to Oman and other regions of Northern Arabia. They are typically tall and dark brown in complexion, and very fierce and powerful in their physique.

2. Secondly, when the Holy Prophet Muḥammad ﷺ received the ordinance to establish fifty prayers a day, Moses ﷺ strongly intervened to lessen the number. He strongly urged the Prophet ﷺ to go back to his Lord a number of times, until the number of obligatory prayers were reduced from fifty to five.

This incident of Prophet Moses' ﷺ intervention on behalf of the Muslims is reported in the authentic sources of the Israa' and Mi'raaj. It illustrates the concern of Moses ﷺ, his friendship and sympathy for the Prophet Muḥammad ﷺ and all Muslims. Prophet Moses ﷺ is also reported to have sobbed out of compassion and sorrow for the Jews, because the followers of Muḥammad ﷺ will enter Paradise in greater numbers than his own.

Imām Al-Ghazali ﷺ *said* that through the Israa' and Mi'raaj, the Prophet Muḥammad's ﷺ surpassing of Moses ﷺ is well confirmed.

For while Prophet Mūsā ﷺ was granted the status of KALĪMULLĀH (the one who talked to Allāh), Prophet Muḥammad ﷺ was granted the vision of Allāh ! He was truly the Chosen Messenger of Allāh, RASŪLALLĀH ﷺ !!

Chapter 25
Prophet Mūsā عليه السلام And The Prayer - Ṣalāh

The ordinance of Muslim prayer (ṢALĀH) was one of the cardinal objectives of Israa' and Mi'raaj. Perhaps it comes next only to the objective of honouring the Prophet, and his consolation by Almighty Allāh after the loss of his beloved wife, the great Khadījah رضي الله عنها, and then of his protector Abū Ṭālib. This tour in the realm of the Divine was certainly the foremost purpose of Israa' and Mi'raaj. These events were meant by Allāh:[101]

... لِنُرِيَهُۥ مِنْ ءَايَٰتِنَآ ...

"...To show him from our great signs".

(Sūrah Al-Israa', 17:1)

When Muḥammad ﷺ saw something of the portents or tokens of his Lord, his heart was consoled and his anxieties about the fate of his call to Islam were allayed. This was because he was shown evidence of the decisive victories of Islam to come in the future.

101 The Holy Qur'ān, Surah Al-Israa', Chapter 37, Ayah 164.

He was shown signs of his Lord's most consummate Omnipotence and grandeur. He was further granted a vision of the Divine Himself. These objectives being realised, the most practical objective was the ordinance of ṢALĀH.

It may be asked, why of all the religious obligations, was Ṣalāh uniquely ordained. It was ordained not on earth but in Heaven, and by Almighty Allāh Himself in person, and not through the Archangel Jibrīl ﷺ ?

The answer to these questions highlight the supreme, central and pivotal significance of Ṣalāh in Islam. We summarise some of these as follows :

1. Ṣalāh is the 'Imād Ad-Deen, the arch-column of Islam.

2. Ṣalāh is the first deed to be assessed and judged on the Day of Reckoning.

3. Ṣalāh is the daily Mi'raaj or spiritual ascent of the Muslim. It is his chief instrument of worship and of sharing in the labour of the angels, namely the singing of the praises of the Lord and of affirming servanthood and submission to His will.

4. Ṣalāh is the means of bringing the Muslim closest to his Lord, Sovereign and Sustainer of the Heavens and the earth and everything therein. When a Muslim is close to his Lord, his prayers will be answered, his worthy hopes and good desires will be granted.

5. Ṣalāh can shield the Muslim from the evil of Satan and his agents, from vice, corruption and lewdness. The Qur'ān says:[102]

... إِنَّ ٱلصَّلَوٰةَ تَنْهَىٰ عَنِ ٱلْفَحْشَآءِ وَٱلْمُنكَرِ ۗ ...

"Surely Ṣalāh restrains (you) from lewdness, and from shameful, evil deeds."

(Sūrah Al-'Ankabūt, 29:45)

6. The Qur'ān also repeatedly commends Ṣalāh as the cardinal weapon of the Muslim, especially in times of hardship and distress. The Qur'ān says :[103]

وَٱسْتَعِينُوا۟ بِٱلصَّبْرِ وَٱلصَّلَوٰةِ ۚ وَإِنَّهَا لَكَبِيرَةٌ إِلَّا عَلَى ٱلْخَٰشِعِينَ ﴿٤٥﴾

"And seek Allāh's help with patient perseverance and Salah; Surely, it (Ṣalāh) is a heavy duty, except for those who are humble."

(Sūrah Al-Baqarah, 2:45)

As mentioned previously, Prophet Moses عليه السلام was instrumental (out of compassion for Prophet Muḥammad ﷺ and his Ummah) in reducing the number of daily prayers from fifty to only five. He repeatedly advised Prophet Muḥammad ﷺ to go back to Almighty Allāh, and ask for a reduction in the number. He told Prophet Muḥammad ﷺ that he had previous experience in this matter with the Israelites who found it very difficult to perform only two prayers, one at dawn and one at sunset. This incident indeed illustrates the affinity that existed between Prophet Moses عليه السلام and Prophet Muḥammad ﷺ, and the close affinity that ought to exist between true Believers of Almighty God.

102 The Holy Qur'ān, Surah Al-'Ankabūt, Chapter 29, Ayah 45.

103 The Holy Qur'ān, Surah Al-Baqarah, Chapter 2, Ayah 45.

Chapter 26
Ṣalāh And The Rationale Of Religion

ṢALĀH is closely related to the rationality of religious life.

If one believes that one is created by Almighty God, who is the one and only Benevolent source of the blessings of life, then to pray to Him is the rational thing to do.

It is only natural to be grateful to one's Creator and Sustainer.

Performing Ṣalāh is the ritual expression of this gratitude.

A person of a naturally wholesome and noble disposition, whose native common sense has not been spoiled by arrogance and false pride, will find it rational as well as commendable to pray, especially in times of hardship.

At the same time, the discipline of Ṣalāh, listening and following the Imām leading the Prayer, attaches the Muslim inwardly to the values of obedience, discipline and socio-political consciousness.

Chapter 27

THE PROPHET ﷺ PREFERS MILK TO WINE

It is reported by Ibn Kathīr and others, that on arriving at Jerusalem, Jibrīl ﷺ offered the Prophet ﷺ two glasses, one containing milk, the other wine. The Prophet ﷺ chose milk. Jibrīl ﷺ commented:

"You have been rightly guided to the natural choice! Had you chosen wine, your Ummah would have been greatly tempted by it".

The choice of milk symbolises an important characteristic of the faith of Islām, namely that it is the natural religion for man, in total harmony with the original, normal disposition of human nature. The Qur'ān calls this original disposition the FITRAH.

According to the Qur'ānic world-view, the human being - man and women - is created by Allāh in a naturally good and pure state, free from sin. This is called the state of FITRAH. A baby at birth is totally innocent. He does not bear the sin or guilt of his parents or ancestors. He starts off with a clean slate. The Qur'ān states :[104]

فَأَقِمْ وَجْهَكَ لِلدِّينِ حَنِيفًا ۚ فِطْرَتَ ٱللَّهِ ٱلَّتِى فَطَرَ ٱلنَّاسَ عَلَيْهَا ۚ لَا تَبْدِيلَ
لِخَلْقِ ٱللَّهِ ۚ ذَٰلِكَ ٱلدِّينُ ٱلْقَيِّمُ وَلَٰكِنَّ أَكْثَرَ ٱلنَّاسِ لَا يَعْلَمُونَ ﴿٣٠﴾

"So set your face (O Muḥammad) for the religion of the naturally upright, (turning away from all that is false) in accordance with natural disposition (Fitrah), in which Allāh has created Mankind. No alteration (let there be) in what Allāh has created. That is the upright religion, but most men know not..."

(Sūrah Ar-Rūm, 30:30)

104 The Holy Qur'ān, Surah Ar-Rūm, Chapter 30, Ayah 30.

Chapter 28
Prophethood Transferred From The Israelites To The Arabs

Ever since Jacob, Prophethood in the region now called the Middle East remained in the house of the Israelites, descendants of Prophet Jacob, son of Isaac, son of Abraham, the Patriarch of the Semitic peoples. Jacob, Joseph and his brothers, then Moses, Aaron, John the Baptist, and Jesus son of Mary, are but a few of the great names.

With the coming of Muḥammad, Prophethood switched from the Israelites to the Arabs, descendants of Ishmael, son of Abraham and Hājar. This change is symbolised in the act in which the Prophet Muḥammad, ushered by Jibrīl, led the prayer, in Masjid Al-Aqṣā, with all the Prophets, including Ādam and Abraham lined up behind him. The Qur'ān gives the reason for this change. The Israelites were initially favoured by Allāh over other people. They succeeded in the holy land of Palestine after the Canaanites, but they did not honour the favour done to them.

Rather, they turned against their Prophets and rebelled against Allāh. They changed and falsified their Scriptures, and killed their Prophets.

In the history of Islām, this change in the fortunes of the Israelites was also symbolised by the change of the Qiblah from Jerusalem to Makkah, an event which marked the beginning of the end of friendship and alliance established between the Muslims and Jews of Madīnah by the pact of ṢAḤĪFAH.

According to the Qur'ān, the Banī Isra'eel are no longer the "chosen people". The Muslim are the best people, but they must fulfil the conditions of being true to the mission of Islam:[105]

كُنتُمْ خَيْرَ أُمَّةٍ أُخْرِجَتْ لِلنَّاسِ تَأْمُرُونَ بِٱلْمَعْرُوفِ وَتَنْهَوْنَ عَنِ ٱلْمُنكَرِ وَتُؤْمِنُونَ بِٱللَّهِ

[...]

"You are the best of peoples raised up for mankind; Enjoining what is right, forbidding what is wrong, and believing in Allāh."

(Sūrah Āli 'Imrān, 3:110)

The link between Israa' and Mi'raaj and the story of the children of Israel is established by the Qur'ān itself. First of all, the Sūrah of Israa' (night journey) is alternately known as the Sūrah of Banī Isra-eel. Secondly, the opening verse of this Sūrah is immediately followed by the mention of Moses ﷺ and Banī Isra-eel, in the following way:

105 The Holy Qur'ān, Surah Āli 'Imrān, Chapter 3, Ayah 110.

وَءَاتَيْنَا مُوسَى ٱلْكِتَٰبَ وَجَعَلْنَٰهُ هُدًى لِّبَنِىٓ إِسْرَٰٓءِيلَ أَلَّا تَتَّخِذُوا۟ مِن دُونِى وَكِيلًا ﴿٢﴾

"We gave unto Moses the Scriptures and appointed it a guidance for the children of Israel, saying: Choose no guardian beside Me".

(Sūrah Al-Israa', 17:2)

This Sūrah of the children of Israel tells about the fate of the ancient Kingdom of the Israelites, after Moses ﷺ; how they spread corruption and arrogance on two occasions, and how Almighty Allāh twice destroyed them, once by the Persians and once by the Romans. Thereafter they were dispersed on the earth (the Diaspora). The Sūrah goes on to set out a rule for the Israelites or Jews:[106]

عَسَىٰ رَبُّكُمْ أَن يَرْحَمَكُمْ ۚ وَإِنْ عُدتُّمْ عُدْنَا ...

"If you return (to your crime of oppression and arrogance), We will return (with Our punishment and chastisement)."

(Sūrah Al-Israa', 17:8)

106 The Holy Qur'ān, Surah Al-Israa', Chapter 17, Ayah 8.

Chapter 29
Socio-Political Dimensions Of Miʿraaj

The event of Miʿraaj marks a watershed in the mission and message of Islām, in the career of the Holy Prophet Muḥammad ﷺ, and in the evolving Islāmic history.

The Prophet's ﷺ Miʿraaj fit in well with the divine scheme in that earlier Prophets, such as Ibrāhīm and Mūsā ﷺ, had undergone a similar experience. Like Prophet Muḥammad ﷺ, they too were provided with an opportunity to gain first hand knowledge of the divine working and secrets of the kingdom of the heavens and the earth:[107]

وَكَذَٰلِكَ نُرِىٓ إِبْرَٰهِيمَ مَلَكُوتَ ٱلسَّمَٰوَٰتِ وَٱلْأَرْضِ وَلِيَكُونَ مِنَ ٱلْمُوقِنِينَ ﴿٧٥﴾

"So also did We show Abraham the kingdom of the heavens and the earth that he might have certitude.

(Sūrah Al-Anʿām, 6:75)

107 The Holy Qur'ān, Surah Al-An ʿām, Chapter 6, Ayah 75.

How Allāh grants life to the dead was vividly demonstrated to Prophet Ibrāhīm ﷺ:[108]

وَإِذْ قَالَ إِبْرَٰهِـۧمُ رَبِّ أَرِنِى كَيْفَ تُحْىِ ٱلْمَوْتَىٰ ۖ قَالَ أَوَلَمْ تُؤْمِن ۖ قَالَ بَلَىٰ وَلَـٰكِن لِّيَطْمَئِنَّ قَلْبِى ۖ قَالَ فَخُذْ أَرْبَعَةً مِّنَ ٱلطَّيْرِ فَصُرْهُنَّ إِلَيْكَ ثُمَّ ٱجْعَلْ عَلَىٰ كُلِّ جَبَلٍ مِّنْهُنَّ جُزْءًا ثُمَّ ٱدْعُهُنَّ يَأْتِينَكَ سَعْيًا ۚ وَٱعْلَمْ أَنَّ ٱللَّهَ عَزِيزٌ حَكِيمٌ ﴿٢٦٠﴾

"Behold! Abraham said: "My Lord! show me how Thou givest life to the dead. He said: "Dost thou not then believe?" He said: "Yea! but to satisfy my own understanding." He said: "Take four birds; tie them (cut them into pieces), then put a portion of them on every hill, and call to them; they will come to thee (flying) with speed. Then know that Allāh is Exalted in Power, Wise."

(Sūrah Al-Baqarah, 2:260)

Prophet Mūsā ﷺ saw Allāh's Glory on the Mount and was granted a unique opportunity to appreciate the divine knowledge:[109]

وَلَمَّا جَآءَ مُوسَىٰ لِمِيقَـٰتِنَا وَكَلَّمَهُۥ رَبُّهُۥ قَالَ رَبِّ أَرِنِىٓ أَنظُرْ إِلَيْكَ ۚ قَالَ لَن تَرَىٰنِى وَلَـٰكِنِ ٱنظُرْ إِلَى ٱلْجَبَلِ فَإِنِ ٱسْتَقَرَّ مَكَانَهُۥ فَسَوْفَ تَرَىٰنِى ۚ فَلَمَّا تَجَلَّىٰ رَبُّهُۥ لِلْجَبَلِ جَعَلَهُۥ دَكًّا وَخَرَّ مُوسَىٰ صَعِقًا ۚ فَلَمَّآ أَفَاقَ قَالَ سُبْحَـٰنَكَ تُبْتُ إِلَيْكَ وَأَنَا۠ أَوَّلُ ٱلْمُؤْمِنِينَ ﴿١٤٣﴾

"When Moses came to the place appointed by Us and his Lord addressed him, He said: "O my Lord! show (Thyself) to me, that I

108 The Holy Qur'ān, Surah Al-Baqarah, Chapter 2, Ayah 260.

109 The Holy Qur'ān, Surah Al-Aʿrāf, Chapter 7, Ayah 143.

may look upon Thee." Allāh said: "By no means canst thou see Me (direct); but look upon the mount; if it abide in its place, then shalt thou see Me." When his Lord manifested Himself to the Mount, He made it as dust, and Moses fell down in a swoon. When he recovered his senses he said: "Glory be to Thee! to Thee I turn in repentance, and I am the first to believe."

(Sūrah Al-Aʿrāf, 7:143)

فَوَجَدَا عَبْدًا مِّنْ عِبَادِنَآ ءَاتَيْنَٰهُ رَحْمَةً مِّنْ عِندِنَا وَعَلَّمْنَٰهُ مِن لَّدُنَّا عِلْمًا ﴿٦٥﴾

"So they found one of Our servants on whom We had bestowed Mercy from Ourselves and whom We had taught knowledge from Our own presence."[110]

(Sūrah Al-Kahf, 18:65)

Miʿraaj signifies a Messenger's elevation to higher ranks and a manifold increase in his responsibilities. After having carried out the mission of Islam for some twelve years, Prophet Muḥammad ﷺ was granted Miʿraaj. By this time he had preached his message throughout the Hijāz and the neighbouring country of Abyssinia. It was time for his mission to enter a new phase. He was soon to move from the hostile environment of Makkah to the friendly environment of Madīnah, which was ready to host his message and mission. Since it was to be a consequential move, transforming the Islamic movement into the Islamic State and exposing Islam to other nations, Allāh summoned the Prophet Muḥammad ﷺ for special instructions. This marvellous journey happened,

110 The Holy Qur'ān, Surah Al-Kahf, Chapter 18, Ayah 65.

significantly enough, only a year before the Prophet's ﷺ Hijrah (migration) to Madīnah.

Why the Prophet ﷺ was summoned for Mi'raaj is set out quite clearly in Sūrah Al-Israa'. In one part of the Sūrah the Makkan unbelievers are warned that if they continue persecuting Muslims and force the Prophet ﷺ into migration, It would ruin the fate of the Makkan unbelievers:[111]

يَوْمَ نَدْعُوا۟ كُلَّ أُنَاسٍۭ بِإِمَـٰمِهِمْ ۖ فَمَنْ أُوتِىَ كِتَـٰبَهُۥ بِيَمِينِهِۦ فَأُو۟لَـٰٓئِكَ يَقْرَءُونَ
كِتَـٰبَهُمْ وَلَا يُظْلَمُونَ فَتِيلًا ﴿٧١﴾ وَمَن كَانَ فِى هَـٰذِهِۦٓ أَعْمَىٰ فَهُوَ فِى ٱلْـَٔاخِرَةِ
أَعْمَىٰ وَأَضَلُّ سَبِيلًا ﴿٧٢﴾ وَإِن كَادُوا۟ لَيَفْتِنُونَكَ عَنِ ٱلَّذِىٓ أَوْحَيْنَآ إِلَيْكَ
لِتَفْتَرِىَ عَلَيْنَا غَيْرَهُۥ ۖ وَإِذًا لَّٱتَّخَذُوكَ خَلِيلًا ﴿٧٣﴾ وَلَوْلَآ أَن ثَبَّتْنَـٰكَ لَقَدْ كِدتَّ
تَرْكَنُ إِلَيْهِمْ شَيْـًٔا قَلِيلًا ﴿٧٤﴾ إِذًا لَّأَذَقْنَـٰكَ ضِعْفَ ٱلْحَيَوٰةِ وَضِعْفَ ٱلْمَمَاتِ
ثُمَّ لَا تَجِدُ لَكَ عَلَيْنَا نَصِيرًا ﴿٧٥﴾ وَإِن كَادُوا۟ لَيَسْتَفِزُّونَكَ مِنَ ٱلْأَرْضِ
لِيُخْرِجُوكَ مِنْهَا ۖ وَإِذًا لَّا يَلْبَثُونَ خِلَـٰفَكَ إِلَّا قَلِيلًا ﴿٧٦﴾ سُنَّةَ مَن قَدْ أَرْسَلْنَا
قَبْلَكَ مِن رُّسُلِنَا ۖ وَلَا تَجِدُ لِسُنَّتِنَا تَحْوِيلًا ﴿٧٧﴾

"One day We shall call together all human beings with their (respective) Imāms: those who are given their record in their right hand will read it (with pleasure), and they will not be dealt with unjustly in the least. (71) But those who were blind in this world, will be blind in the Hereafter, and most astray from the Path. (72) And their purpose was to tempt thee away from that which We had revealed unto thee, to substitute in Our name something quite different: (in that case), behold! they would certainly have made thee (their) friend! (73) And had We not given thee strength, thou wouldst nearly have inclined to them a little. (74) In that case We

111 The Holy Qur'ān, Surah Al-Israa', Chapter 17, Ayah 71-77.

should have made thee taste an equal portion (of punishment) in this life, and an equal portion in death: and moreover thou wouldst have found none to help thee against Us! (75) Their purpose was to scare thee off the land, in order to expel thee; but in that case they would not have stayed (therein) after thee except for a little while. (76) (This was Our) way with the messengers We sent before thee: thou wilt find no change in Our ways. (77)"

(Sūrah Al-Israa', 17:71-77)

And the followers of Prophet Mūsā ﷺ who were present in the Hijāz, and who were to interact with the Prophet in Madīnah, were told that it was their last chance to mend their ways in that they had already wasted earlier opportunities:[112]

وَقَضَيۡنَآ إِلَىٰ بَنِيٓ إِسۡرَٰٓءِيلَ فِي ٱلۡكِتَٰبِ لَتُفۡسِدُنَّ فِي ٱلۡأَرۡضِ مَرَّتَيۡنِ وَلَتَعۡلُنَّ عُلُوّٗا
كَبِيرٗا ٤ فَإِذَا جَآءَ وَعۡدُ أُولَىٰهُمَا بَعَثۡنَا عَلَيۡكُمۡ عِبَادٗا لَّنَآ أُوْلِي بَأۡسٖ شَدِيدٖ
فَجَاسُواْ خِلَٰلَ ٱلدِّيَارِۚ وَكَانَ وَعۡدٗا مَّفۡعُولٗا ٥ ثُمَّ رَدَدۡنَا لَكُمُ ٱلۡكَرَّةَ عَلَيۡهِمۡ
وَأَمۡدَدۡنَٰكُم بِأَمۡوَٰلٖ وَبَنِينَ وَجَعَلۡنَٰكُمۡ أَكۡثَرَ نَفِيرًا ٦ إِنۡ أَحۡسَنتُمۡ أَحۡسَنتُمۡ
لِأَنفُسِكُمۡۖ وَإِنۡ أَسَأۡتُمۡ فَلَهَاۚ فَإِذَا جَآءَ وَعۡدُ ٱلۡأٓخِرَةِ لِيَسُـُٔواْ وُجُوهَكُمۡ وَلِيَدۡخُلُواْ
ٱلۡمَسۡجِدَ كَمَا دَخَلُوهُ أَوَّلَ مَرَّةٖ وَلِيُتَبِّرُواْ مَا عَلَوۡاْ تَتۡبِيرًا ٧ عَسَىٰ رَبُّكُمۡ أَن
يَرۡحَمَكُمۡۚ وَإِنۡ عُدتُّمۡ عُدۡنَاۚ وَجَعَلۡنَا جَهَنَّمَ لِلۡكَٰفِرِينَ حَصِيرًا ٨

"And We gave (clear) warning to the Children of Israel in the Book, that twice would they do mischief on the earth and be elated with mighty arrogance (and twice would they be punished)! (4) When the first of the warnings came to pass, We sent against you Our servants given to terrible warfare: they entered the very inmost parts of your homes; and it was a warning (completely) fulfilled. (5) Then did

112 The Holy Qur'ān, Surah Al-Israa', Chapter 17, Ayah 4-8.

We grant you the Return as against them: We gave you increase in resources and sons, and made you the more numerous in manpower. (6) If ye did well ye did well for yourselves; if ye did evil, (ye did it) against yourselves; so when the second of the warnings came to pass (We permitted your enemies) to disfigure your faces, and to enter your Temple as they had entered it before and to visit with destruction all that fell into their power. (7) It may be that your Lord may (yet) show Mercy unto you; but if ye revert (to your sins), We shall revert (to Our punishments): and We have made Hell a prison for those who reject (all Faith). (8)"

(Sūrah Al-Israa', 17:4-8)

The main thrust of the Sūrah, however, consists in laying down the following fourteen fundamental principles which form the foundation of human conduct, morals and culture:

1. Allāh alone is to be worshipped and no partners be ascribed to Him:[113]

وَقَضَىٰ رَبُّكَ أَلَّا تَعْبُدُوٓا۟ إِلَّآ إِيَّاهُ وَبِٱلْوَٰلِدَيْنِ إِحْسَـٰنًا ۚ إِمَّا يَبْلُغَنَّ عِندَكَ ٱلْكِبَرَ أَحَدُهُمَآ أَوْ كِلَاهُمَا فَلَا تَقُل لَّهُمَآ أُفٍّ وَلَا تَنْهَرْهُمَا وَقُل لَّهُمَا قَوْلًا كَرِيمًا ﴿٢٣﴾

"Thy Lord hath decreed that ye worship none but Him, and that ye be kind to parents. Whether one or both of them attain old age in thy life, say not to them a word of contempt, nor repel them, but address them in terms of honour."

(Sūrah Al-Israa', 17:23)

113 The Holy Qur'ān, Surah Al-Israa', Chapter 17, Ayah 23.

2. The family should hold pride of place in the society. Children should be obedient to parents and due rights be rendered to the kindred:[114]

وَٱخْفِضْ لَهُمَا جَنَاحَ ٱلذُّلِّ مِنَ ٱلرَّحْمَةِ وَقُل رَّبِّ ٱرْحَمْهُمَا كَمَا رَبَّيَانِى
صَغِيرًا ﴿٢٤﴾ رَّبُّكُمْ أَعْلَمُ بِمَا فِى نُفُوسِكُمْ إِن تَكُونُوا۟ صَٰلِحِينَ فَإِنَّهُۥ
كَانَ لِلْأَوَّٰبِينَ غَفُورًا ﴿٢٥﴾ وَءَاتِ ذَا ٱلْقُرْبَىٰ حَقَّهُۥ [...]

"And, out of kindness, lower to them the wing of humility, and say: "My Lord! bestow on them thy Mercy even as they cherished me in childhood." Your Lord knoweth best what is in your hearts: If ye do deeds of righteousness, verily He is Most Forgiving to those who turn to Him again and again (in true penitence). And render to the kindred their due rights [...]"

(Sūrah Al-Israa', 17:24-26)

3. The poor, the wayfarer, and the needy must be helped:[115]

[. . .] وَٱلْمِسْكِينَ وَٱبْنَ ٱلسَّبِيلِ [. . .]

[...] as (also) to those in want, and to the wayfarer: [...]

(Sūrah Al-Israa', 17:26)

4. One should not squander his wealth. For spendthrifts are brothers of Satan:[116]

... وَلَا تُبَذِّرْ تَبْذِيرًا ﴿٢٦﴾
إِنَّ ٱلْمُبَذِّرِينَ كَانُوٓا۟ إِخْوَٰنَ ٱلشَّيَٰطِينِ ۖ وَكَانَ ٱلشَّيْطَٰنُ لِرَبِّهِۦ كَفُورًا ﴿٢٧﴾

114 The Holy Qur'ān, Surah Al-Israa', Chapter 17, Ayah 24-26.
115 The Holy Qur'ān, Surah Al-Israa', Chapter 17, Ayah 26.
116 The Holy Qur'ān, Surah Al-Israa', Chapter 17, Ayah 26-27.

"[...] But squander not (your wealth) in the manner of a spendthrift. Verily spendthrifts are brothers of the Evil Ones; and the Evil One is to his Lord (himself) ungrateful."

(Sūrah Al-Israa', 17:26-27)

5. One should be moderate in his expenditure in that one should be neither wasteful nor miserly. For it puts others to hardship too:[117]

إِنَّ ٱلْمُبَذِّرِينَ كَانُوٓاْ إِخْوَٰنَ ٱلشَّيَٰطِينِ ۖ وَكَانَ ٱلشَّيْطَٰنُ لِرَبِّهِۦ كَفُورًا ﴿٢٧﴾

"Verily spendthrifts are brothers of the Evil Ones; and the Evil One is to his Lord (himself) ungrateful."

(Sūrah Al-Israa', 17:27)

وَلَا تَجْعَلْ يَدَكَ مَغْلُولَةً إِلَىٰ عُنُقِكَ وَلَا تَبْسُطْهَا كُلَّ ٱلْبَسْطِ فَتَقْعُدَ مَلُومًا مَّحْسُورًا ﴿٢٩﴾

"Make not thy hand tied (like a miser's) to thy neck, nor stretch it forth to its utmost reach, so that thou become blameworthy and destitute."

(Sūrah Al-Israa', 17:29)

6. Man should not disturb the divine arrangement for distributing sustenance. Man does not have the capability to do this job:[118]

117 The Holy Qur'ān, Surah Al-Israa', Chapter 17, Ayah 27 and 29.

118 The Holy Qur'ān, Surah Al-Israa', Chapter 17, Ayah 30.

إِنَّ رَبَّكَ يَبْسُطُ ٱلرِّزْقَ لِمَن يَشَآءُ وَيَقْدِرُ ۚ إِنَّهُۥ كَانَ بِعِبَادِهِۦ خَبِيرًۢا
بَصِيرًا ﴿٣٠﴾

"Verily thy Lord doth provide sustenance in abundance for whom He pleaseth, and He provideth in a just measure. For He doth know and regard all His servants."

(Sūrah Al-Israa', 17:30)

7. One should not kill one's children for fear of want. For Allāh will provide sustenance for them as He does for us:[119]

وَلَا تَقْتُلُوٓا۟ أَوْلَـٰدَكُمْ خَشْيَةَ إِمْلَـٰقٍ ۖ نَّحْنُ نَرْزُقُهُمْ وَإِيَّاكُمْ ۚ إِنَّ قَتْلَهُمْ كَانَ
خِطْـًٔا كَبِيرًا ﴿٣١﴾

"Kill not your children for fear of want: We shall provide sustenance for them as well as for you. Verily the killing of them is a great sin."

(Sūrah Al-Israa', 17:31)

8. Illicit sex is an abhorrent way of fulfilling one's desire. Not only should one shun it as a sin, any approach or temptation to it should be avoided as well:[120]

وَلَا تَقْرَبُوا۟ ٱلزِّنَىٰٓ ۖ إِنَّهُۥ كَانَ فَـٰحِشَةً وَسَآءَ سَبِيلًا ﴿٣٢﴾

"Nor come nigh to adultery: for it is a shameful (deed) and an evil, opening the road (to other evils)."

(Sūrah Al-Israa', 17:32)

119 The Holy Qur'ān, Surah Al-Israa', Chapter 17, Ayah 31.
120 The Holy Qur'ān, Surah Al-Israa', Chapter 17, Ayah 32.

9. Allāh has sanctified human life. No one should therefore be killed except for just cause. Nor should anyone commit suicide:[121]

وَلَا تَقْتُلُوا۟ ٱلنَّفْسَ ٱلَّتِى حَرَّمَ ٱللَّهُ إِلَّا بِٱلْحَقِّ ۗ وَمَن قُتِلَ مَظْلُومًا فَقَدْ جَعَلْنَا لِوَلِيِّهِۦ سُلْطَـٰنًا فَلَا يُسْرِف فِّى ٱلْقَتْلِ ۖ إِنَّهُۥ كَانَ ﴿٣٣﴾

"Nor take life - which Allāh has made sacred - except for just cause. And if anyone is slain wrongfully, we have given his heir authority (to demand qiṣāṣ or to forgive): but let him not exceed bounds in the matter of taking life; for he is helped (by the Law).

(Sūrah Al-Israa', 17:33)

10. The orphans' interest should be carefully safeguarded until they come of age:[122]

. . وَلَا تَقْرَبُوا۟ مَالَ ٱلْيَتِيمِ إِلَّا بِٱلَّتِى هِىَ أَحْسَنُ حَتَّىٰ يَبْلُغَ أَشُدَّهُۥ . . .

"And come not nigh to the orphan's property except to improve it, until he attains the age of full strength;"

(Sūrah Al-Israa', 17:34)

11. One should keep his word or promise, because one is accountable to Allāh for all deeds:[123]

. . . وَأَوْفُوا۟ بِٱلْعَهْدِ ۖ إِنَّ ٱلْعَهْدَ كَانَ مَسْـُٔولًا ﴿٣٤﴾

121 The Holy Qur'ān, Surah Al-Israa', Chapter 17, Ayah 33.

122 The Holy Qur'ān, Surah Al-Israa', Chapter 17, Ayah 34.

123 The Holy Qur'ān, Surah Al-Israa', Chapter 17, Ayah 35.

". . . and fulfil (every) engagement, for (every) engagement will be enquired into (on the Day of Reckoning)."

(Sūrah Al-Israa', 17:34)

12. One should give just measure and weight:

وَأَوْفُوا۟ ٱلْكَيْلَ إِذَا كِلْتُمْ وَزِنُوا۟ بِٱلْقِسْطَاسِ ٱلْمُسْتَقِيمِ ۚ ذَٰلِكَ خَيْرٌ وَأَحْسَنُ تَأْوِيلًا ﴿٣٥﴾

"Give full measure when you measure, and weigh with a balance that is straight: that is the most fitting and the most advantageous in the final determination."

(Sūrah Al-Israa', 17:35)

13. Idle curiosity and following one's whims are to be avoided. He will have to answer how he has used his abilities and power:[124]

وَلَا تَقْفُ مَا لَيْسَ لَكَ بِهِۦ عِلْمٌ ۚ إِنَّ ٱلسَّمْعَ وَٱلْبَصَرَ وَٱلْفُؤَادَ كُلُّ أُو۟لَٰٓئِكَ كَانَ عَنْهُ مَسْـُٔولًا ﴿٣٦﴾

"And pursue not that of which thou hast no knowledge; for every act of hearing, or of seeing or of (feeling in) the heart will be enquired into (on the Day of Reckoning)."

(Sūrah Al-Israa', 17:36)

14. Arrogance, insolence or pride is to be shunned. For it

124 The Holy Qur'ān, Surah Al-Israa', Chapter 17, Ayah 36.

is the first step to many evils:

وَلَا تَمْشِ فِى ٱلْأَرْضِ مَرَحًا ۖ إِنَّكَ لَن تَخْرِقَ ٱلْأَرْضَ وَلَن تَبْلُغَ ٱلْجِبَالَ طُولًا ۝٣٧

"Nor walk on the earth with insolence: for thou canst not rend the earth asunder, nor reach the mountains in height."[125]

(Sūrah Al-Israa', 17:37)

Far from being mere moral precepts, these fourteen principles, revealed to the Prophet Muḥammad ﷺ on the Mi'raaj night, were to serve as the very manifesto of Islam. They signified the foundation of the Islamic order of Life.

The Prophet ﷺ was presented with this set of guidelines at the time his mission was about to assume the role of political power and state. Understandably, he was instructed in advance on what principles the society was to be built.

In addition to this guidance, Almighty Allāh enjoined upon all Muslims to pray five times a day in order to strengthen morally and spiritually those entrusted with following this guidance.

Prayers were prescribed for them lest they become oblivious of Allāh. For Prayers would keep them ever-conscious of their role as servants of Allāh, answerable to Him for all their deeds.

125 The Holy Qur'ān, Surah Al-Israa', Chapter 17, Ayah 37.

PART SEVEN

IMPACT OF THE ISRAA'
WAL MI'RAAJ

Chapter 30
Impact Of The Israa' And Mi'raaj

The event of Israa' and Mi'raaj has always had a deep and lasting impact on the thought and life of Muslims, and was echoed by many writers and philosophers. Countless poets and story-tellers have eternalized the event.

In the Muslim world, to this day, the Israa' and Mi'raaj is commemorated in festivals, feasts, and sessions of religious teaching about its significance.

The poet-philosopher, Abūl 'Alā' Al-Ma'arrī, wrote his celebrated Risālah Al-Ghufan expressing his impressions of the fantastic sights the Holy Prophet ﷺ beheld during his ascent to the heavens. In particular, the terrible torments of the people of Hell, and the amazing bliss of the people of Paradise.

The poet-mystic Ibn Al-Fārid wrote beautiful verses about the elevation of the Holy Prophet Muḥammad ﷺ, how he drew near to his Lord, surpassing all angels and Prophets.

Ibn Al-'Arabī wrote Shajarat Al-Kawn – The Tree of the Cosmos – in which he mentioned the greatness of this event.

European poets and writers were also drawn to the fascination and extraordinary beauty of the event.

The best known among them is Dante Alighieri who is said to have based his "Divine Comedy" on this event.

For Muslims at large, the Israa' and Mi'raaj signify above all, Almighty Allāh's bestowal of grace on His Prophet and Messenger, Rasūlallāh ﷺ.

And his confirmation as the Imām and leader of the spiritual realm, of Angels and Jinns, as well as Prophets.

Imām Al-Busayri رحمه الله composer of the great poem, Al-Burdah Ash-Sharīf (*Ode of the Prophetic Mantle*), said in this respect:

> "You journey by night from a sacred mosque to a sacred mosque, as a moon steals its way in the darkness of night ... Ascending, ascending till you reached such heights, so near to the Divine as none had attempted before ..."

The Sudanese poet, Wad Sa'ad, comparing the station achieved by the Holy Prophet ﷺ through the Israa' and Mi'raaj, and that achieved by Prophet Mūsā عليه السلام when Almighty Allāh spoke to him at Sinai, said:

> "The son of 'Imrān (*Moses*) عليه السلام traversed a sea seen by the naked eye, but the Chosen One (*Muḥammad Al-Mustafa* ﷺ) traversed the sea of heaven, closely guarded and surrounded by Angels."

Chapter 31

Poems On The Miʿraaj

FĪ LAYLATIN TATAZAYYĀ QASĪDATUL ISRAA' WAL MI'RAAJ[126]

[CHORUS]

FĪ LAYLATIN TATAZAYYĀ — BIN- NŪRI WAL ISH-RĀQI
JIBRĪLU JĀ'AN- NABĪYĀ — YAD'ŪHU FAWQAL- BURĀQI

HUWAN- NABĪYUL- AMĪNU — LAHUṢ- ṢA'ĀBU TAHŪNU
FA QAWLUHU QAWLA ŞIDQIN — WA FI'LUHU MA'MŪNU

AJIB NIDĀ-AS-SAMĀ'I — YĀ SAYYIDAL ANBIYĀ'I
YAR'ĀKA RABBAL BARĀYĀ — FĪ RIHLATIL ISRĀ'I

WA ḤĪNA TAMMAL WUSŪLU — FIL QUDSI ṢALLAR- RASŪLU
WA KĀNA KHAYRU RAFĪQIN — LIL MUṢṬAFĀ JIBRĪLU

ṢALLŪ 'ALAL- MUHKTĀRI — YUḤĀṬU BIL- ANWĀRI
'INDAL- LADHĪ NARTAJĪHI — QAD FĀZA BIL-ASRĀRI

QAD 'ĀDA YAḤMILU FARḌAN — KHAMSAN MIN ṢALAWĀTIN
WA YAMNAḤUL- ARḌA FAYḌAN — KHAYRAN MIN BARAKĀTIN

WA 'ĀDA FAWQAL BURĀQI — MIN FAWQI SAB'IN ṬIBĀQIN
YAD'Ū LIMAN SADDAQŪHU — BIL- FAWZI YAWMAT- TALĀQI

126 www.ShaykhFaisal.com/QasidahMiraajunNabi

قَصِيدَةُ الإسِرَاءِ والمِعْرَاج

فِي لَيْلَةٍ تتزَيَّا ... بِالنُّورِ وَالْإِشْرَاقِ
جِبْرِيلُ جَاءَ اَلنَّبِيَّ ... يَدْعُوهُ فَوْقَ اَلْبُرَاقِ

هُوَ اَلنَّبِيُّ اَلْأَمِينُ ... لَهُ اَلصِعَابُ تُهُونُ
فَقَوْلُهُ قَوْلَ صِدْقٍ ... وَفِعْلُهُ مَأْمُونُ

أَجِبْ نِدَاءَ السَّمَاءِ ... يَا سَيِّدَ الْأَنْبِيَاءِ
يَرْعَاكَ رَبَّ البَرَايَا ... فِي رِحْلَةِ الْإِسِرَاءِ

ووَحِينَ تَمَّ اَلْوُصُولُ ... فِي اَلْقُدْسِ صَلَّى الرَّسُولُ
وَكَانَ خَيْرُ رَفِيقٍ ... لِلْمُصْطَفَى جِبْرِيلُ

صَلُّوْا عَلَى اَلْمُخْتَارِ ... يُحَاطُ بِالْأَنْوَارِ
عِنْدَ اَلَّذِي نَرْتَجِيهِ ... قَدْ فَازَ بِالْأَسْرَارِ

قَدْ عَادَ يَحْمِلُ فَرْضًا ... خَمْسًا مِنْ صَلَوَاتٍ
وَيَمْنَحُ الْأَرْضَ فَيْضًا ... خَيْرًا مِنْ بَرَكَاتٍ

وَعَادَ فَوْقَ اَلْبُرَاقِ ... مِنْ فَوْقِ سَبْعِ طِبَاقٍ
يَدْعُوا لِمَنْ صَدَّقُوهُ ... بِالْفَوْزِ يَوْمَ اَلتَّلَاقِ

From "Mathnawi" of Imām Ar-Rūmī

The moon traverses the constellations
of the zodiac in a single night,
So why do you deny the Miʿraaj (Ascension)?
That wondrous, unique Pearl (the Holy Prophet)
is like a hundred moons – for when
He made one gesture, the moon was split
in two.

And the marvel that he displayed
in splitting the moon
Was in keeping with the weakness
of the creatures' perception.
The work and business of the Prophets
and Messengers
Is beyond the spheres and the stars.
Transcend the spheres and their revolution!
Then you will see that work and business."

Qasīdah Al-Burdah Al-Sharīfah of Imām Al-Busayri

SECTION 7 OF THE BURDAH
Concerning the Mi'raaj of Rasūlallāh Ṣallallāhu 'Alayhī Wa Sallam

يَا خَيْرَ مَنْ يَمَّمَ العَافُونَ سَاحَتَهُ
سَعْيًا وَفَوْقَ مُتُونِ الأَيْنُقِ الرُّسُمِ

O you the best of those to whose court seekers of bounties resort;
Running and mounted on the backs of fast camels.

وَمَنْ هُوَ الآيَةُ الكُبْرَى لِمُعْتَبِرٍ
وَمَنْ هُوَ النِّعْمَةُ العُظْمَى لِمُغْتَنِمِ

And O you who is the greatest sign for he who takes a lesson;
And O you who is the greatest bounty for a person who avails himself of it.

سَرَيْتَ مِنْ حَرَمٍ لَيْلاً إِلَى حَرَمِ
كَمَا سَرَى البَدْرُ فِي دَاجٍ مِنَ الظُّلَمِ

You travelled by night from one sacred place to another;
As the full moon travels through intense darkness.

وَبِتَّ تَرْقَى إِلَى أَنْ نِلْتَ مَنْزِلَةً
مِنْ قَابِ قَوْسَيْنِ لَمْ تُدْرَكْ وَلَمْ تُرَمِ

And you continued ascending until you attained a position;
At the distance of two cubits length, as has never been attained nor sought.

وَقَدَّمَتْكَ جَمِيعُ الأَنْبِيَاءِ بِهَا
وَالرُّسْلِ تَقْدِيمَ مَخْدُومٍ عَلَى خَدَمِ

And you were preferred due to your position by all the Anbiyya (Prophets),
And Rasūls (Messengers), just as a servant gives preference to his master.

وَأَنْتَ تَخْتَرِقُ السَّبْعَ الطِّبَاقَ بِهِمْ
فِي مَوْكِبٍ كُنْتَ فِيهِ الصَّاحِبَ العَلَمِ

You passed the seven heavens with them,
In a procession in which you were the standard bearer.

حَتىَّ إِذَا لَمْ تَدَعْ شَأْوًا لِمُسْتَبِقٍ
مِنَ الدُّنُوِّ وَلاَ مَرْقًى لِمُسْتَنِمِ

Until you left no goal for any competitor to strive for.
In closeness, nor any room for ascent for any to advance.

خَفَضْتَ كُلَّ مَقَامٍ بِالإِضَافَةِ إِذْ
نُودِيْتَ بِالرَّفْعِ مِثْلَ المُفْرَدِ العَلَمِ

You made inferior every position by your advance, when
You were invited to His majestic and unique position.

كَيْمَا تَفُوزَ بِوَصْلٍ أَيِّ مُسْتَتِرٍ
عَنْ العُيُونِ وَسِرٍّ أَيِّ مُكْتَتَمِ

So that you may be successful in a reaching the most concealed,
From all eyes and secrets well concealed.

فَحُزْتَ كُلَّ فَخَارٍ غَيْرَ مُشْتَرَكٍ
وَجُزْتَ كُلَّ مَقَامٍ غَيْرَ مُزْدَحَمِ

So you acquired every (status) worthy of pride unrivalled,
And you surpassed every position, which none other surpassed.

وَجَلَّ مِقْدَارُ مَا وُلِّيتَ مِنْ رُتَبٍ
وَعَزَّ إِدْرَاكُ مَا أُولِيْتَ مِنْ نِعَمِ

And extremely excellent are the ranks that were granted to you,
And incomprehensible are those bounties that were conferred upon you.

بُشْرَى لَنَا مَعْشَرَ الإِسْلاَمِ إِنَّ لَنَا
مِنَ العِنَايَةِ رُكْنًا غَيْرَ مُنْهَدِمِ

Glad tiding be to us O people of Islam! We have
By the grace of Allāh a pillar which is indestructible.

لَمَّا دَعَا اللهُ دَاعِينَا لِطَاعَتِهِ
بِأَكْرَمِ الرُّسْلِ كُنَّا أَكْرَمَ الأُمَمِ

When Allāh called the one who invited us (Rasūlallāh) to His worship;
Because of the Noblest of Messengers, we are the noblest of Ummats.

Chapter 32
Miʿraaj In The Light Of Science

Almighty Allāh says in the Holy Qur'ān:[127]

سُبْحَانَ الَّذِيْ أَسْرَى بِعَبْدِهِ لَيْلاً مِنَ الْمَسْجِدِ الْحَرَامِ إِلَى الْمَسْجِدِ الأَقْصَى الَّذِيْ بَارَكْنَا حَوْلَهُ لِنُرِيَهُ مِنْ آيَاتِنَا إِنَّهُ هُوَ السَّمِيْعُ الْبَصِيْرُ ۝١

"Glory be to Allāh who took His servant for a journey by night from the Sacred Mosque to the Farthest Mosque, whose precincts We did bless. In order that We might show him some of Our signs. For He is the One who sees and hears (all things)."

(Sūrah Al-Israa', 17:1)

Almighty Allāh showed the Holy Prophet ﷺ many great signs on this momentous journey to the heavens.[128] The Blessed Prophet

127 The Holy Qur'ān, Surah Al-Israa', Chapter 17, Ayah 1.

128 Dr. Kazim Ebrahim: Essays on Islamic Topics, The Islamic Academy, Port-of-Spain, Trinidad, West Indies, 1993.

Muḥammad ﷺ made many statements about scientific issues. Some of these were proven by scientists long after the time of the Prophet, while other statements are still being investigated waiting for new scientific evidence to prove them. Amazingly, none of his statements were proven wrong![129]

The Prophet ﷺ was transported in a flying object called "Burāq", which had the shape of an animal the size of which was between a mule and a donkey, and which shot into space with the speed of light at 186,282 miles per second or even faster. Burāq comes from the Arabic word Barq which means lightning.

Is it possible that the Prophet ﷺ was transported to another "dimension" different from the linear time we are accustomed to?

The present day Television set can show images in two dimensions, i.e. length and breath. Depth is a third dimension and time is a fourth dimension. The technology of today can record our actions, not our thoughts. But, the Holy Prophet ﷺ mentioned the complete and total recording of all our actions and the consequences of good deeds and bad deeds.

The earth rotates on its axis at a speed of 1037 miles per hour (MPH) at the equator. (We are constantly moving at twice the speed of a jet plane and we don't even feel it.) The earth takes a day to move once on its axis. A year is the time it takes the earth to travel once around the sun, at a speed of 66,672 MPH in an elliptical orbit. With the earth rotating on its axis at 1037 MPH

The Author (Shaykh Faiṣal) met Dr. Kazim Ebrahim on a previous visit to Trinidad and Tobago.

129 Dr. Kazim Ebrahim: Essays on Islamic Topics, The Islamic Academy, Port-of-Spain, Trinidad, West Indies, 1993.

and around the sun at 66,672 MPH, when viewed from outer space, the earth and other planets are seen to "swim" or "float" in space. The Holy Qur'ān mentions that the celestial bodies swim along or float, each in its rounded course.

Many other scientific facts are associated with this remarkable event of Mi'raaj.

Chapter 33
Commemorating The Occasion

Educational Programs

Lectures, Seminars and Workshops can be organised to educate Muslims and Non-Muslims about this miraculous occasion.

These programs can be held in Masjids, Islamic Centres, homes, or any other appropriate places. The entire family (parents and children) should be encouraged to participate.

This is an excellent opportunity to educate the community about the Seerah (Life History) of the Holy Prophet Muḥammad ﷺ, peace and blessings of Allāh be upon him, and especially about this Great Miracle that was given to the Holy Prophet ﷺ by Almighty Allāh.

Ṣalāt And Salām - Invocating Blessings And Peace Upon The Holy Prophet Muḥammad ﷺ

This is also an occasion to remind ourselves of the importance of sending Salāt and Salām upon the beloved Prophet ﷺ. This is an act of worship ('Ibādah) which Muslims should engage in everyday of their lives.

Almighty Allāh reveals to us in the Holy Qur'ān:

إِنَّ ٱللَّهَ وَمَلَٰٓئِكَتَهُۥ يُصَلُّونَ عَلَى ٱلنَّبِيِّۚ يَٰٓأَيُّهَا ٱلَّذِينَ ءَامَنُواْ صَلُّواْ
عَلَيۡهِ وَسَلِّمُواْ تَسۡلِيمًا ٥٦

"Verily, Allāh and His angels shower blessings on the Prophet, O you who believe! Ask blessings on him and salute him with a worthy salutation."

(Sūrat Al-Aḥzāb, 33:56)

There are many Aḥadīth which mention the importance and virtues of Salāt and Salām. Some of these are given below.

Anas ؓ reported that the Messenger of Allāh ﷺ said:

> "If anyone sends Ṣalāt upon me once, Allāh will reward him with ten blessings, ten sins will be remitted from him, and he will be raised ten degrees."
> **(An-Nasā'i)**

> Abū Hurayrah reported that the Messenger of Allāh ﷺ said:
>
> > "If anyone sends Ṣalāt upon me once, Allāh will bless him ten times."
> > **(Muslim)**

ʿAbdullāh Ibn Masʿūd ؓ reported that the Messenger of Allāh ﷺ said:

> "The one who will be nearest to me on the Day of Judgement is the one who was most frequent in sending Ṣalāt (Darūd)

upon me."
(At-Tirmidhi)

Resources For This Occasion Of Miʿraajun Nabi:

PALESTINE IN ISLAM LECTURE SERIES

www.ShaykhFaisal.com/PalestineSeries

QASIDATUL ISRAA' WAL MIʿRAAJ

www.ShaykhFaisal.com/QasidahMiraajunNabi

Glossary of Islamic Terms

ADHĀN The call to Prayer (Ṣalāh).

AḤĀDĪTH (Plural of Ḥādīth), Reports of the sayings, deeds and actions approved by the Holy Prophet Muḥammad ﷺ.

AL-BAYTUL MAʿMŪR The Oft-Visited House, which is a mirror of the Kaʿbah located in heaven frequently visited by the angels.

ʿĀMUL ḤUZN The Year of Grief, which was marked by the deaths of Khadījah and Abū Ṭālib, and increased persecution of Muslims.

ARCHANGEL JIBRĪL The angel who brought revelation to the Prophet Muḥammad ﷺ and who accompanied him during his Israa' and Miʿraaj.

BANŪ HASHIM An arab clan within the Quraysh to which the Prophet Muḥammad ﷺ and his close relatives belonged.

BANŪ ISRAA-EEL The Arabic term refering to the Jewish people. Isrāeel refers to the Prophet Yaʿqoub, the son of the Prophet Isḥāq, the son of the Prophet Ibrahīm.

BASMALAH	The formula: "BISMILLAHIR RAḤMANIR RAḤĪM".
BAYT LAḤM	The town in Jerusalem where Prophet 'Isā (Jesus) ﷺ was born. (Bethlehem)
BURĀQ	A creature that carried the Holy Prophet ﷺ from Masjidul Ḥaram to Masjidul Aqṣā.
DU'Ā'	A supplication to Allāh ﷻ, or asking Allāh ﷻ for forgiveness, blessing, and mercy, etc.
EID	A day of celebration: Eid-ul-Fitr comes after the end of the Holy Month of Ramadān. Eid-ul-Aḍha occurs during the Hajj season in the Islamic month of Dhul-Hijjah.
FAJR	Name of the Ṣalāh at dawn.
GHUSL	Washing the whole body for Tahārah (cleanliness and purification).
ḤADĪTH	(Plural is Aḥādīth), Reports of the sayings, deeds and actions approved by the Holy Prophet Muḥammad ﷺ.
ḤALĀL	That which is lawful (permitted) in Islam.

ḤARĀM That which is unlawful (forbidden) in Islam.

HIDAYAH Guidance from Almighty Allāh.

ḤIJĀMAH The process of drawing blood from the body by scarification (scratches or superficial incisions in the skin) and the application of a cupping glass (in which a partial vacuum is created, as by heat) for relieving internal congestion and other benefits.

'IBĀDAH Translated as 'worship', it refers to any permitted activity performed to gain the Pleasure of Almighty Allāh ﷻ.

IMĀM A leader, or the person who leads prayer in a congregation.

ĪMĀN Faith or Belief.

ISRAA' The miraculous night journey of Prophet Muḥammad ﷺ from Mecca to Jerusalem, during which he was carried on a winged creature called Burāq.

JAHANNAM Hell or Hellfire – the place of eternal suffering.

JANNAH Heaven or Paradise – the place of eternal bliss. Literally it means 'garden'.

JERUSALEM (Also known as Al-Quds Ash-Shareef) The third holiest city to Muslims in the world. Located in Palestine.

KĀFIR A person who does not believe in Islam.

MADĪNAH The city to which the Prophet Muḥammad ﷺ migrated, the second holiest city to Muslims in the world. Previously known as Yathrib.

MA'RUF Right actions. Its opposite is Munkar or wrong actions.

MASJID AL-AQṢĀ The mosque in Jerusalem, which was the first Qiblah (direction of prayer) of Muslims before it was changed to the Ka'aba in Makkah.

MI'RAAJ The miraculous bodily ascension of Prophet Muḥammad ﷺ to the heavens.

NAFL The plural is Nawāfil. Optional, for example optional prayers.

QAḌĀ' Making up for a missed prayer.

QURAYSH A powerful and influential group of tribes which reside in or surrounding the Holy City of Makkah.

RAFRAF The Mode of transportation used by the Holy Prophet ﷺ after Sidratul Muntahā.

RAKʿAH A 'unit' of Ṣalāh. Each Ṣalāh consists of two, three or four Rakʿahs.

SAJDATUS SAHW The two prostrations to correct a mistake made during Ṣalāh.

ṢALĀH The Islamic ritual prayer that Muslims perform five times a day, which was ordained to the Prophet Muḥammad ﷺ during his Miʿraaj.

SIDRATUL MUNTAHĀ The Lote Tree of the Utmost Boundary, which is the furthest point of the cosmos and serves as a demarcation point.

TAʿAWWUDH Saying "AʿŪDHU BILLĀHI MINASH SHAYTĀNIR RAJĪM".

TAHAJJUD Optional Ṣalāh performed after Ṣalātul ʿIshā' until Dawn or Fajr.

ṬĀ'IF	A city near Makkah, to which the Prophet Muḥammad ﷺ traveled to seek support and protection, but was met with rejection and persecution.
TAKBĪR	Saying "Allāhu Akbar".
TAKBĪRATUL IḤRĀM	Saying Allāhu Akbar at the beginning of Ṣalāh.
TARĀWĪḤ	The special Ṣalāh, consisting of twenty Rak'ahs, performed after Ṣalātul 'Ishā' during the Holy Month of Ramadān.
UMMAH	A nation or a group of people.
WĀJIB	Obligatory, for example an obligatory act of worship such as Ṣalātul Witr.
WITR	Literally means 'odd' (opposite of even), and refers to the Salāh offered after 'Ishā'.
WUḌŪ'	Washing for Ṣalāh in the prescribed way.
ZUHR	Name of the Ṣalāh just after midday.

References

1. The Holy Qur'an : English translation of the meanings and Commentary, A.Yusuf Ali.

2. Sahih Al Bukhari.

3. Sahih Muslim.

4. Ibn Katheer, Al-Hafez: Tafseer Ibn Katheer, Dar Al-Maʿrifah, Beirut.

5. Qutb, Al-Shaheed Sayyid: Fee Zilaal Al Qur'an.

6. Ash-Shaʿraawi, Muhammad Mutawalli: Al-Israaʾ Wal Miʿraaj, edited by Riyad Abdullah, Dar Al-ʿAlam, Beirut, 1985.

7. Bashier, Zakaria: The Makkan Crucible, Islamic Foundation, Leicester, UK, 1978.

8. Bashier, Zakaria: Sunshine at Madīnah, Islamic Foundation, Leicester, UK, 1990.

9. Al-Ghazali. Imam Abu Hamid: Mishkaat Al-Anwaar, Dar Al-Kutub Al-ʿIlmiyyah, Beirut, 1986.

10. At-Turabi, Hassan: As-Salaah ʿImaad Ad-Deen, Kuwait, 1968.

11. Hamid, Abdul Wahid: Islam the Natural Way, MELS, London, 1989.

12. Siddiqui, Abdul Hameed: The Life Of Muhammad, Kazi Publications, Lahore, Pakistan, 1969.

13. Hajjaj, Abdullah: Al-Israaʾ Wal Miʿraaj, Dar Al-Taqwa, London, UK, 1989.

14. Kazim, Ebrahim: Essays on Islamic Topics, The Islamic Academy, Trinidad, West Indies, 1993.

General Ijāzah

This is the text of the GENERAL IJĀZAH received by Shaykh Faisal Hamid Abdur-Razak.

FROM: H.E. AL-'ALLĀMAH AL-SHEIKH MUHAMMAD ABUL HUDA IBN IBRĀHĪM AL-YAQOUBI AL-HASANI [HAFIZAHUL-LĀH]

DATE: THURSDAY - RAMADAN – 15 – 1420 / DECEMBER – 23 - 1999

PLACE: TORONTO – ONTARIO – CANADA.

ARABIC TEXT OF GENERAL IJĀZAH

اَلإِجَازَةُ الْعَامَةُ

اَلْحَمْدُ للهِ الَّذِيْ شَرَّفَ الأُمَّةَ الْمُحَمَّدِيَّةَ بِالإِسْنَادِ وَبَوَّأَ مَنِ اصْطَفَاهُ مِنْ خَلْقِهِ رُتْبَةَ

الْعِلْمِ وَالإِرْشَادِ

...وَالصَّلاَةُ وَالسَّلاَمُ مُتَوَاتِرَانِ مُتَسَلْسِلاَنِ إِلَى النَّبِيِّ صَلَّى اللهُ عَلَيْهِ وَآلِهِ وَسَلَّمَ

... أَمَّا بَعْد

فَقَدْ سَمِعَ مِنِّيْ الْعَالِمُ الْفَاضِلُ وَالْمُهَذَّبُ الْكَامِلُ الْفَقِيْهُ الدَّاعِيَّةُ إِلَى اللهِ تَعَالَى

الشَّيْخُ فَيْصَل حَامِد عَبْدُ الرَّزَّاق

حَدِيْث الرَّحْمَةِ الْمُسَلْسَلَةِ بِالأَوَّلِيَّةِ وَهُوَ أَوَّلُ حَدِيْثٍ سَمِعَهُ مِنِّيْ فِيْ مَدِيْنَةِ تُوْرَنْتُوْ

مِنْ بِلاَدِ كَنَدَا وَذَلِكَ فِيْ ١٥ مِنْ شَهْرِ رَمَضَان مِنْ عَامِ ١٤٢٠ ،

وَقَدْ أَجَزْتُهُ بِرِوَايَتِهِ

كَمَا أَجَزْتُهُ بِرِوَايَةِ الْجَامِعِ الصَّحِيْحِ لِلإِمَامِ الْبُخَارِيِّ وَصَحِيْحِ الإِمَامِ مُسْلِمِ وَمُوَطَّأ

الإِمَامِ مَالِكِ وَسَائِرِ السُّنَنِ وَالصِّحَاحِ وَالْمَسَانِيْد وَالْمَعَاجِم وَالأَجْزَاء وَالْفَهَارِس وَالأَثْبَاتِ بِالإِعْتِمَادِ عَلَى الأُصُوْلِ الصَّحِيْحَةِ ،

وَأَجَزْتُهُ بِتَدْرِيْسِ الْفِقْه الْحَنَفِيّ وَرِوَايَةِ كُتُبِهِ

كَمَا أَجَازَنِيْ بِذَلِكَ مُفْتِي الشَّامِ الْعَلاَّمَة الطَّبِيْب الشَّيْخ مُحَمَّد أَبُوْ الْيُسْرِ عَابِدِيْن (١٤٠١) – ١٣٠٧

عَنْ وَالِدِهِ مُفْتِي الشَّامِ الشَّيْخ مُحَمَّد أَبِي الْخَيرِ عَابِدِيْن (ت ١٣٤٥)

وَجَدِّهِ أَمِيْن الْفَتْوَى السَّيِّد أَحْمَد بن عَبْد الْغَنِيِّ عَابِدِيْن (ت ١٣٠٧)

إِجَازَةً بِرِوَايَةِ السَّيِّدِ أَحْمَد عَنْ عَمِّهِ خَاتِمَةِ الْمُحَقِّقِيْن الْعَلاَّمَة السَّيِّد مُحَمَّد أَمِيْن بن عمر الْمَعْرُوْف بِابن عَابِدِيْن صَاحِبِ الْحَاشِيَّةِ الشَّهِيْرَةِ الْمسماة رَدّ الْمُحْتَارِ وَصَاحِبِ تَنْقِيْحِ الْفَتَاوَى الْحَامِدِيَّةِ وَالرَّسَائِلِ وَغَيْرِهَا بِأَسَانِيْدِهِ الْمَبْسُوْطَةِ فِيْ ثَبْتِهِ الْمُسَمَّى عُقُوْد اللآلِ فِيْ الأَسَانِيْدِ الْعَوَالِي ،

وَعَنْ غَيْرِهِ مِنَ الشُّيُوْخِ وَالْعُلَمَاءِ الَّذِيْنَ أَجَازُوْنِيْ وَأَوَّلهمْ سَيِّدِيْ وَوَلِيِّ فهمي وَوَالِدِيْ الْعَلاَّمَة الشَّيْخ إِبْرَاهِيْم بن إِسْمَاعِيْل الْيَعْقُوْبِي (ت ١٤٠٦).

وَأَسْأَلُ اللهُ تَعَالَى لِلأَخِ الْفَاضِلِ التَّوْفِيْقِ وَالإِخْلاَصِ رَاجِيًا مِنْهُ الدُّعَاء لِيْ

وَلأَشْيَاخِيْ مُوْصِيًا إِيَّاهُ بِالتَّثبت وَالْمُرَاجَعَةِ وَهُوَ شَرْطُ الإِجَازَةِ وَبِخَاصَة عِنْدَ

الْفَتْوَى ،

نَفَعَنَا اللهُ بِبَرَكَاتِ رِجَالِ هَذِهِ الأَسَانِيْدِ وَبَرَكَاتِ الأَوْلِيَاءِ وَالْعُلَمَاءِ الْعَامِلِيْنَ ، إِنَّهُ

. سَمِيْعٌ مُجِيْبٌ

قَالَهُ بِفَمِهِ وَرَقمه بِقَلَمِهِ

أَحْقَرَ الْوَرَى وَأَصْغَرَ من ترى

الْمُتَشَرِّف بِاسْمِ مُحَمَّد

أَبُوْ الْهُدَى الْيَعْقُوْبِي الْحَسَنِي

. فِيْ مَدِيْنَةِ تُوْرَنْتُوْ مِنْ بِلادِ كَنَدَا بِأَمْرِيْكَا الشِّمَالِيَّة

رَمَضَان / ١٤٢٠ / ١٨

ISNĀD ḤADĪTH AR-RAḤMAH

[ARABIC TEXT OF ISNĀD]

إِسْنَادُ حَدِيْثِ الرَّحْمَة

حَدَّثَنَا الْعَلاَّمَةُ الشَّيْخُ مُحَمَّدٌ أَبُوْ الْهُدَى ابن إِبْرَاهِيْم ابن إِسْمَاعِيْل الْيَعْقُوْبِيُّ

الْحَسَنِيُّ ،

وَهُوَ أَوَّلُ حَدِيْثٍ سَمِعْتُهُ مِنْهُ ، قَالَ

حَدَّثَنَا الْعَلاَّمَةُ الشَّيْخُ مُحَمَّدٌ الْمَكِّيُّ الْكَتَّانِيُّ الْحَسَنِيُّ ،

مُفْتِيْ الْمَالِكِيَّةِ فِيْ دِمَشْقَ (ت ١٣٩٣) ،

: وَهُوَ أَوَّلُ حَدِيْثٍ سَمِعْتُهُ مِنْهُ ، قَالَ

حَدَّثَنَا الْعَلاَّمَةُ السَّيِّدُ أُحْمَد بن إِسْمَاعِيْل الْبَرْزَنْجِيُّ الْحَسَنِيُّ (ت ١٣٣٧) ،

مُفْتِيْ الشَّافِعِيَّةِ فِيْ الْمَدِيْنَةِ الْمُنَوَّرَةِ ،

وَهُوَ أَوَّلُ حَدِيْثٍ سَمِعْتُهُ مِنْهُ ، قَالَ

حَدَّثَنَا وَالِدِيْ الْعَلاَّمَةُ السَّيِّدُ إِسْمَاعِيْل بن زَيْن الْعَابِدِيْن الْبَرْزَنْجِيُّ الْحَسَنِيُّ

، (ت ١٢٨١)

وَهُوَ أَوَّلُ حَدِيْثٍ سَمِعْتُهُ مِنْهُ ، قَالَ:

عَنْ الشَّيْخ صَالِح بن مُحَمَّد الْعُمَرِيِّ الْفُلاَّنِيِّ (ت ١٢١٨) ،

وَهُوَ أَوَّلُ حَدِيْثٍ سَمِعْتُهُ مِنْهُ ، قَالَ:

عَنْ الشَّمْسِ مُحَمَّد بن مُحَمَّد الْمَغْرِبِيِّ (ت ١٢٠٥) ،

: وَهُوَ أَوَّلُ حَدِيْثٍ سَمِعْتُهُ مِنْهُ ، قَالَ:

عَنْ مُسْنِدِ الْحِجَازِ عَبْدِ اللهِ بن سَالِمِ الْبَصْرِيِّ (ت ١١٣٤) ،

وَهُوَ أَوَّلُ حَدِيْثٍ سَمِعْتُهُ مِنْهُ ، قَالَ:

عَنْ الْحَافِظِ مُحَمَّد بن عَلاءِ الدِّيْنِ الْبَابِلِيِّ (ت ١٠٧٧) ،

وَهُوَ أَوَّلُ حَدِيْثٍ سَمِعْتُهُ مِنْهُ ، قَالَ:

عَنْ سَالِمِ بن مُحَمَّد السَّهْنُوْرِيِّ (ت) ،

وَهُوَ أَوَّلُ حَدِيْثٍ سَمِعْتُهُ مِنْهُ ، قَالَ:

عَنْ نَجْمِ الدِّيْنِ مُحَمَّد بن أَحْمَد الْغَيْطِيِّ (ت) ،

وَهُوَ أَوَّلُ حَدِيْثٍ سَمِعْتُهُ مِنْهُ ، قَالَ:

عَنْ الْجَمَالِ يُوْسُف بن زَكَرِيا بن مُحَمَّد الأَنْصَارِيِّ (ت) ،

: وَهُوَ أَوَّلُ حَدِيْثٍ سَمِعْتُهُ مِنْهُ ، قَالَ:

عَنْ أَبِيْهِ شَيْخِ الإِسْلاَمِ زَكَرِيا بن مُحَمَّد الأَنْصَارِيِّ (ت ٩٢٦) ،

وَهُوَ أَوَّلُ حَدِيْثٍ سَمِعْتُهُ مِنْهُ ، قَالَ:

عَنْ خَاتِمَةِ الْحُفَّاظِ أَحِمَد بن عَلِيٍّ ابن حَجَرِ الْعَسْقَلاَنِيِّ (ت ٨٥٢) ،

وَهُوَ أَوَّلُ حَدِيْثٍ سَمِعْتُهُ مِنْهُ ، قَالَ:

عَنْ الْحَافِظِ وَلِيّ الدِّيْنِ عَبْد الرَّحِيْم بن الْحُسَيْنِيِّ الْعِرَاقِيِّ (ت) ،

وَهُوَ أَوَّلُ حَدِيْثٍ سَمِعْتُهُ مِنْهُ ، قَالَ:

عَنْ صَدْرِ الدِّيْنِ مُحَمَّد بن مُحَمَّد بن إِبْرَاهِيْم الْمَيْدُوْمِيِّ (ت) ،

وَهُوَ أَوَّلُ حَدِيْثٍ سَمِعْتُهُ مِنْهُ ، قَالَ:

عَنْ أَبِيْ النَّجِيْبِ عَبْد المُنْعِم ابن الصَّيْقَلِ الْحَرَّانِيِّ (ت) ،

وَهُوَ أَوَّلُ حَدِيْثٍ سَمِعْتُهُ مِنْهُ ، قَالَ:

عَنْ الْحَافِظِ أَبِيْ الْفَرَجِ عَبْد الرَّحْمنِ بن عَلِيٍّ ابن الْجَوْزِيِّ (ت) ،

وَهُوَ أَوَّلُ حَدِيْثٍ سَمِعْتُهُ مِنْهُ ، قَالَ:

عَنْ أَحْمَد بن إِسْمَاعِيْل أَبِيْ صَالِح بن عَبْد المَلِكِ الْمُؤَذِّنِ النَّيْسَابُوْرِيِّ (ت) ،

وَهُوَ أَوَّلُ حَدِيْثٍ سَمِعْتُهُ مِنْهُ ، قَالَ:

عَنْ أَبِيْهِ أَبِيْ صَالِح إِسْمَاعِيْل بن عَبْد المَلِكِ الْمُؤَذِّنِ النَّيْسَابُوْرِيِّ (ت) ،

وَهُوَ أَوَّلُ حَدِيْثٍ سَمِعْتُهُ مِنْهُ ، قَالَ:

عَنْ أَبِيْ طَاهِر مُحَمَّد بن مُحَمَّد بن مَحْمِشٍ (بِوَزْنِ مَسْجِدٍ) الزِّيَادِيِّ (ت) ،

وَهُوَ أَوَّلُ حَدِيْثٍ سَمِعْتُهُ مِنْهُ ، قَالَ:

عَنْ أَبِيْ حَامِد أَحْمَد بن مُحَمَّد بن يَحْيَى بن بِلاَلِ الْبَزَّازِ (ت) ،

وَهُوَ أَوَّلُ حَدِيْثٍ سَمِعْتُهُ مِنْهُ ، قَالَ:

عَنْ عَبْدِ الرَّحْمن بن بِشْرِ بن الْحَكَمِ الْعَبدِيِّ (ت ٢٦٠) ،

وَهُوَ أَوَّلُ حَدِيْثٍ سَمِعْتُهُ مِنْهُ ، قَالَ:

عَنْ أَمِيْرِ الْمُؤْمِنِيْنَ سُفْيَان بن عُيَيْنَةَ (ت) ،

وَهُوَ أَوَّلُ حَدِيْثٍ سَمِعْتُهُ مِنْهُ ، قَالَ:

عَنْ عَمْرُو بن دِيْنَارِ (ت) ،

وَهُوَ أَوَّلُ حَدِيْثٍ سَمِعْتُهُ مِنْهُ ، قَالَ:

عَنْ أَبِيْ قَامُوْس مَوْلَى سَيِّدِنَا عَبْدِ اللهِ بن عَمْرو بن العَاصِ (ت) ،

وَهُوَ أَوَّلُ حَدِيْثٍ سَمِعْتُهُ مِنْهُ ، قَالَ:

عَنْ سَيِّدِنَا عَبْدِ اللهِ بن عَمْرو بن العَاصِ (ت) ،

قَالَ سَمِعْتُ رَسُوْلَ اللهِ صَلَّى اللهُ عَلَيْهِ وَسَلَّمَ يَقُوْلُ:

الرَّاحِمُوْنَ يَرْحَمُهُمُ الرَّحْمنُ تَبَارَكَ وَتَعَالَى

ارْحَمُوْا مَنْ فِيْ الأَرْضِ يَرْحَمُكُمْ مَنْ فِيْ السَّمَاءِ

. بِرَفْعِ (يَرْحَمُكُمْ) عَلَى الدُّعَاءِ ، وَجَزْمِهِ جَوَاباً لِلطَّلَبِ

. وَأَرْوِيْهِ عَنْ نَحْوِ ثَلاَثِيْنَ مِنَ الشُّيُوْخِ بِأَسَانِيْدَ أُخْرَى

ISNĀD ḤADĪTH AR-RAḤMAH

[TRANSLITERATION]

HAD-DA-THANĀ AL-'AL-LĀMAH AL-SHAYKH MUHAMMAD ABUL HUDA IBN IBRĀHĪM IBN ISMĀ'ĪL AL-YA'QOUBI AL-HASANI

WA HUWA AW-WALU HADĪTHIN SAMI'TUHU MINHU, QĀLA

HAD-DA-THANĀ AL-'AL-LĀMAH AL-SHAYKH MUHAMMAD AL-MĀLIKĪY AL-KATTĀNĪY AL-HASANĪY MUFTI AL-MĀLIKIYYAH FĪ DIMASHQA (TAWAFFĀ 1393H)

WA HUWA AW-WALU HADĪTHIN SAMI'TUHU MINHU, QĀLA

HAD-DA-THANĀ AL-'AL-LĀMAH AL-SAYYID AHMAD IBN ISMĀ'ĪL AL-BARZANJIYYU AL-HUSAYNIYYU (TAWAFFĀ 1337H) MUFTI AL-SHĀFI'IYYATI FIL- MADĪNATIL- MUNAWWARATI

WA HUWA AW-WALU HADĪTHIN SAMI'TUHU MINHU, QĀLA

HAD-DA-THANĀ WĀLIDĪ AL-SAYYID ISMĀ'ĪL IBNU ZAYNIL- 'ĀBIDĪN AL-BARZANJIYYU (TAWAFFĀ 1281H)

WA HUWA AW-WALU HADĪTHIN SAMI'TUHU MINHU,

'AN AL-SHAYKH SĀLIH IBNI MUHAMMADIN AL-'UMARIYYI AL-FULLĀNĪYI (TAWAFFĀ 1218H)

WA HUWA AW-WALU HADĪTHIN SAMI'TUHU MINHU,

'AN AL-SHAMSI MUHAMMADIN IBNI MUHAMMADIN AL-MAGHRABIYYI (TAWAFFĀ 1205)

WA HUWA AW-WALU HADĪTHIN SAMI'TUHU MINHU,

'AN MUSNIDIL- HIJĀZI 'ABDILLĀHI IBNI SĀLIMI AL-BASRIYYI (TAWAFFĀ 1134H)

WA HUWA AW-WALU HADĪTHIN SAMI'TUHU MINHU,

'AN AL-HĀFIZ MUHAMMADIN IBN 'ALĀ-ID-DĪN AL-BĀBILIYYI

WA HUWA AW-WALU HADĪTHIN SAMI'TUHU MINHU,

'AN SĀLIMIN IBNI MUHAMMADIN AL-SAHNŪRIYYI

WA HUWA AW-WALU HADĪTHIN SAMI'TUHU MINHU,

'AN NAJMIDDĪNI MUHAMMADIN IBNI AHMADIN AL-GHAYṬĪ

WA HUWA AW-WALU HADĪTHIN SAMI'TUHU MINHU,

'AN AL-JAMĀL YUSUF IBNI ZAKARIYYA AL-ANSĀRIYYI

WA HUWA AW-WALU HADĪTHIN SAMI'TUHU MINHU,

'AN ABĪHI SHAYKHUL ISLĀM ZAKARIYYA IBNI MUHAMMADIN AL-ANSĀRIYYI

WA HUWA AW-WALU HADĪTHIN SAMI'TUHU MINHU,'AN KHĀTIMATIL HUFFĀZ AHMAD IBN 'ALI IBN HAJAR AL-'ASQALĀNI (TAWAFFĀ 852H)

WA HUWA AW-WALU HADĪTHIN SAMI'TUHU MINHU,

'AN AL-HĀFIZ WALIYUDDIN 'ABDUR RAHIM IBN AL-HUSAYNIY AL-'IRĀQI

WA HUWA AW-WALU HADĪTHIN SAMI'TUHU MINHU,

'AN SADRUDDIN MUHAMMAD IBN MUHAMMAD IBN IBRĀHĪM AL-MAYDŪMIYYI

WA HUWA AW-WALU HADĪTHIN SAMI'TUHU MINHU,

'AN ABIN-NAJĪB 'ABDUL MUN'IM IBN AL-SAYQALI AL-HARRĀNIY

WA HUWA AW-WALU HADĪTHIN SAMI'TUHU MINHU,

'AN AL-HĀFIZ ABIL FARAJ 'ABDUR-RAHMĀN IBN 'ALI IBN AL-JAWZIYYI (TAWAFFĀ 597H)

WA HUWA AW-WALU HADĪTHIN SAMI'TUHU MINHU,

'AN AHMAD IBN ISMĀ'ĪL ABI SĀLIH ABDUL-MALIK AL-MU-ADH-DHINI AN-NAYSĀBŪRĪ

WA HUWA AW-WALU HADĪTHIN SAMI'TUHU MINHU,

'AN ABĪHI ABĪ SĀLIH ISMĀ'ĪL IBN ABDUL-MALIK AL-MU-ADH-DHINI AN- NAYSĀBŪRĪ (TAWAFFĀ 470H)

WA HUWA AW-WALU HADĪTHIN SAMI'TUHU MINHU,

'AN ABĪ TĀHIR MUHAMMAD IBN MUHAMMAD IBN MAHMISHIN (BI WAZNI MASJIDIN) AL-ZIYĀDĪY (TAWAFFĀ 410H)

WA HUWA AW-WALU HADĪTHIN SAMI'TUHU MINHU,

'AN ABĪ HĀMIDIN AHMAD IBN MUHAMMAD IBN YAHYA IBN BILĀL AL-BAZZĀZ (TAWAFFĀ 330H)

WA HUWA AW-WALU HADĪTHIN SAMI'TUHU MINHU,

'AN ABDIR-RAHMĀN IBN BISHRI IBN AL-HAKAMI AL-'ABDIYYI (TAWAFFĀ 260H)

WA HUWA AW-WALU HADĪTHIN SAMI'TUHU MINHU,

'AN AMIRIL MU'MINĪNA SUFYĀN IBN 'UYAYNATA

WA HUWA AW-WALU HADĪTHIN SAMI'TUHU MINHU,

‘AN ‘AMRIN IBN DINĀRIN

WA HUWA AW-WALU HADĪTHIN SAMI‘TUHU MINHU,

‘AN ABĪ QĀMŪSI MAWLA SAYYIDINA ‘ABDILLĀH IBN ‘AMR IBNAL ‘ĀS

WA HUWA AW-WALU HADĪTHIN SAMI‘TUHU MINHU,

‘AN SAYYIDINA ‘ABDILLAH IBN ‘AMR IBNAL ‘ĀS, QĀLA

SAMI‘TU RASŪLLALĀHI [SALLALLĀHU ‘ALAYHI WA SALLA-MA] YAQŪL:

AR-RĀHIMŪNA YARHAMUHUMUR- RAHMĀNU TABĀRAKA WA TA‘ĀLĀ, IRHAMŪ MAN FIL ARDI YARHAMUKUM MAN FIS-SAMĀ’I

BI-RAF‘I (YARHAMUKUM) ‘ALAD- DU‘Ā’I, WA JAZMIHI JAWĀBAN LIT-TALABI
WA ARWĪHI ‘AN NAHWI THALĀTHĪNA MINASH- SHUYŪKHI BI-ASĀNĪDA UKHRĀ.

Books Written By Shaykh Faisal

ShaykhFaisal.com/AlWirdulAam

ShaykhFaisal.com/BlessingsOfIstighfar

ShaykhFaisal.com/BlessingsOfSalawat

ShaykhFaisal.com/BendicionesDelSalawat

ShaykhFaisal.com/RamadanCompanion

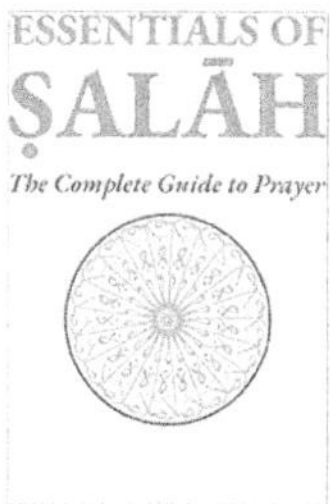

ShaykhFaisal.com/EssentialsOfSalah

All books can be purchased from **www.ShaykhFaisal.com/Author**

Shaykh Faisal has authored numerous titles in the Islamic Sciences. A summary list is provided below.

Qurʾānic Sciences

- Tafsīr Sūrah Al-Fātiḥah
- Tafsir Al-Qurʾān Al-Karīm
- Tajwid Al-Qurʾān Al-Karīm

Arabic Language

- Teach Yourself Arabic Reading
- Teach Yourself Arabic Calligraphy
- Help Yourself to Read Qurʾān
- Arabic Languages for Beginners (Level One)
- Arabic Languages for Beginners (Level Two)

Ḥadīth Sciences

- Gems of Prophetic Wisdom
- Actions are by Intentions

ʿAqīdah (Islamic Creed & Theology)

- Sharh Al-ʿAqīdah Aṭ-Ṭaḥāwiyyah (Commentary of the Aqīdah of Imām Aṭ-Ṭaḥāwi)

Fiqh (Islamic Jurisprudence)

- Nūr Al-Iḍāḥ (The Clarifying Light): A Manual of Ḥanafī Fiqh
- Kitāb Aṣ-Ṣalāh (A Manual of Prayer)

- Kitāb Al-Mawt (The Book of Death)
- Kitāb Al-Ṭahāra (The Book of Purity)
- Kitāb An-Nikāḥ (the Book of Marriage)
- Kitāb Al-Ḥajj (A Manual of Ḥajj and ʿUmrah)
- Essentials of Ṣalāh: The Complete Guide to Prayer

Taṣawwuf (Islamic Spirituality)

- Al-Wirdul ʿAam: The General Litany for Purification, Blessings & Spiritual Elevation
- Blessings of Ṣalawāt: Upon the Holy Prophet Muḥammad ﷺ
- Blessings of Istighfār: Seeking Forgiveness from Almighty Allāh ﷻ
- Blessings of Taḥlīl
- Commentary of Al-Wirdul ʿAam
- Ramaḍān Companion: Spiritual Reflections
- Dhikrullāh: The Remembrance of Allāh
- Kitāb Ad-Duʿā' (Manual of Supplications)

Seerah of the Prophet ﷺ

- Sīrah Muḥammadur Rasūlallāh: Life of the Messenger of Allāh ﷺ
- Milād An-Nabī ﷺ

Islamic Lifestyle

- On Love and Marriage

About the Author

His Eminence Shaykh Faiṣal Ḥāmid 'Abdur-Razāk is an Islāmic Scholar, authorized Spiritual Guide (Murshid), public speaker, teacher, and author. From 1977 to 1985 the Shaykh spent nine years studying the traditional Sacred Sciences in Makkah and Jeddah. Since then, he has continued pursuing sacred knowledge in Damascus, Syria as well as Morocco, Türkiye, Malaysia, Pakistan, India, the United Kingdom, the United States, and Canada. He has received Ijāzah from many distinguished Shaykhs and eminent scholars. He has authored over twenty-five books that remain practical staples for seekers and students alike. He also holds a degree from York University in Canada.

Shaykh Faiṣal is a recognized Shaykh of Taṣawwuf authorized as a Murshid by His Eminence Al- 'Allāmah Shaykh Muḥammad Ibn Ibrāhim Ibn Ismā'il Al-Ya'qoubi Al-Hasani Al-Idrisi (Ḥafiẓahullah). He took the Shādhilī Tarīqah from the great Shaykh and serves as his Global Spiritual Representative (Khalīfah). Shaykh Faiṣal is the Murshid of the Shādhilī Ṭarīqah based out of Canada where he guides and instructs his Murīds all over the world. Among his numerous recognitions as an authoritative Sunni Sufi Scholar, the Shaykh has received 'The Most Prominent Taṣawwuf Scholar' award from the former Prime Minister of Malaysia — The Esteemed Mahathir Mohamad.

The Shaykh began his journey for sacred knowledge in 1977, he studied at Umm Al-Qura University in Makkah and King Abdul-Aziz University in Jeddah. Complimenting his formal education, he took the Sacred Sciences from Great Scholars of the region including: As-Sayyid Shaykh Muḥammad ibn 'Alawi Al-Māliki Al-Ḥasani, Shaykh Muḥammad 'Alī Al-Sabūnī, Shaykh Ḥasan Ayūb, Shaykh Muḥammad Al-Ghazālī, Shaykh Muḥammad Qutb, Shaykh 'Abdur-Raḥman Barood, Shaykh Muḥammad Al-Wasfi, Shaykh Farooq Al-Batal, Shaykh 'Abdullah Nasih 'Alwa, Maw'il Ezziddin Al-Samura'ee and many other distinguished scholars.

About the Publisher

Al-Faiṣaliyyah Press is the official publishing arm of the Islamic Forum of Canada, Al-Faiṣaliyyah Islamic School, and our Spiritual Ṭarīqah. Our team is dedicated to publishing the authored texts and literary works of Shaykh Faiṣal Hāmid Abdur-Razāk.

Please contact us directly for all purchasing inquiries of acquiring distribution copies of the author's works. You can also consider purchasing from Amazon in Canada, the USA, the UK, and all other international Amazon Marketplaces.

All books can be purchased from:

www.ShaykhFaisal.com/Author

For all inquiries, suggestions, and comments please contact:

Media@IslamicForumOnline.com

(905) 790-8859

Visit our online portals for further information:

www.IslamicForumOnline.com

www.ShaykhFaisal.com

Connect with us on our Social Media Pages:

www.YouTube.com/ShaykhFaisal/LIVE

www.Facebook.com/ShaykhFaisal

www.Instagram.com/ShaykhFaisal

www.Twitter.com/ShaykhFaisal

Printed in Great Britain
by Amazon

39795773R00139